ACCELERATE

THE **FAST TRACK** TO SORT YOUR **BOOKS**, SORT YOUR **BUSINESS**, SORT YOUR **LIFE**

KERI WHITELAW

First published 2026

Published by Drive Press

ISBN: 978-1-7642513-3-4 (paperback)
978-1-7642513-4-1 (ebook)

NATIONAL LIBRARY OF AUSTRALIA

A catalogue record for this book is available from the National Library of Australia

Acknowledgements

My journey to becoming a BAS agent began back in 1999. As I was about to become a new mum, the new world of GST was also about to begin. This is where I'd like to acknowledge Danny Tighe, an accountant I worked with many years ago, who encouraged me to register. The rest is history!

SYB – Sort Your Books isn't just me. It has become what it is today through the wonderful employees who have worked alongside me throughout this journey and helped shape the business into what it is today.

I'm a big believer in meditation, affirmations, writing goals and achieving them. Through meditation, ideas often come to me, and I bring them to my team, who take them on board and help make them happen. Without them helping guide the roadmap, SYB wouldn't be what it is today.

Zane Whitelaw – now a chartered accountant, for being an amazing bookkeeper during his uni years. Sarah Ilic and Jade Chasemore, while they are no longer with SYB, have both been a meaningful part of our story and assisted to get SYB to where it is today. Jane St Quintin I truly appreciate the support, encouragement and contribution that you have given over the years.

Karen Ashton-Bradley what can I say – you are the ying to my yang. Without you this book and this business we work in wouldn't be what it is today! Your support and encouragement helps me keep on going. You truly are the most amazing person. I love working with you and feel blessed that I am able to create a space where we can work, grow and change the world together!

To Jane Anderson. Back in 2024 I decided to attend a Content Creation Bootcamp. Why? No idea really – I just liked to write. I wasn't planning on writing a book, but I was writing a weekly blog, so I decided to head off to Kingscliff and do the two-day course. Jane helped to set things in place for me to complete the content that would eventually form this book. Pink sheets. So many pink sheets! But it wasn't only the pink sheets that she introduced me to, but also the wonderful people that attend Jane's courses and are in her world. It's a fantastic environment to be a part of – one where she supports us in a beautiful ecosystem where we can grow and be all that we can be. Thank you Jane for setting me off on the track that would end up with *Accelerate*.

While this book has my name as the author, there are a lot of people who have helped me to become who I am today and who I have to say thank you as well. First, my family. My hubby Sime (36 years this year)! Thank you for sitting beside me, supporting me through thick and thin, offering your opinion and all the other things you do for me. To my sons Zane and Aaryn, who I love and adore, and to Taylah – Aaryn's fiance – thanks for doing all that you do! (You know what I'm talking about.) And to my Mum and Dad, and my brother Gav, I hope that by reading this book, you'll get to know what I do!

To those that helped put the book together – Kristen Lowrey – somehow you interpreted my work and made my words sing, and

Sylvie Blaire from a simple discussion you created the most beautiful book cover.

Last but not least to my Aunty Colleen Morgan who did some much needed research for me along with the proofreading. I'm truly blessed and forever grateful for all that you've done to help me bring this book to life!

To my clients past and present, I thank you for trusting me and my team with your bookwork and your numbers. We're all about connection and we love to have a chat. I hope that this book sparks something in you to find out more and delve deeper into your numbers.

Dedicated to Tania May Hiku

Table of Contents

Introduction

You might not love numbers, but you likely know they matter. As a business owner numbers are in the background of every decision you make. Cash flow. Pricing. Payroll. Tax. Growth. Sometimes they're under control, and sometimes they're not, but they can often be a source of low-level (or not so low-level) stress.

If you're thinking about starting a business, the numbers can feel even heavier. You might be wondering, *how much profit do I need each month? What do I charge?* Or, *when will I actually start making some money!*

Most people struggle with their numbers not because they're bad at business, but because no one ever taught them how to understand their numbers in a way that feels natural.

This book exists to change that one.

Why this book and why now?

There are a lot of business books out there. So why this one? Why now?

Because the world of being in business is changing faster than ever, especially for those of us in bookkeeping, accounting and the numbers game. AI is shifting the way we work, the way we serve and the way we show up. And because of that understanding your numbers just isn't optional anymore. It's vital to succeeding in a fast-paced, changing business environment.

This book is my way of *accelerating* your understanding by handing you the simple tips and gentle nudges that keep you at the forefront of your business, quiet the noise and not be overwhelmed by it. Of course, we'll talk numbers, starting with your own magic number. (And if you're saying, 'Magic and numbers?' Yes, they can co-exist and do!)

You'll discover what your breakeven is – that is, when you'll actually start making money. You'll learn how to use financial reports for insights and better decision making, how to improve pricing and cash flow awareness and even how to connect your business performance with your personal life outcomes for the better.

We'll also explore what accounting tools and AI can actually do for you as a business owner, and how to weave them into your everyday world in practical, human ways. I'll share how financial experts automate efficiently and safely and show you how to embrace technology to accelerate your business and financial success.

Throughout the book you'll see that I often use the term 'bookkeeper' to mean a registered BAS agent. This is simply to keep it easy to read (registered BAS agent is quite a mouthful when repeated over and over!). However, it's important to understand that there is a difference between a registered BAS agent in terms of qualifications, registration and the services they are legally allowed to provide. Registered BAS agents are registered with the Tax Practitioners Board and are authorised to provide BAS services for a fee while a bookkeeper is not.

Being in business isn't only about systems and tech. It's also about balance, taking a moment and knowing when enough is enough. Throughout the book, I'll share insights and stories from real business owners about how understanding their numbers helped them make better decisions and move forward with more confidence so they could stay grounded even while they were reaching and striving for more!

Most importantly, we'll do it together with fun and heart, and a focus on the human side of the numbers game. Years ago a co-worker said to me, 'You know, Keri... you're not like other numbers people.'

I laughed and asked what he meant.

He said, 'You've actually got a personality. You like a laugh.' At the time I wasn't sure how to take it, but now I get it. I'm a people person. I love a chat! And you'll find that same vibe in this book. No drama – just straight talk and a clear pathway forward to a better understanding of where you are, and where you can be, in your business.

In a world that isn't standing still and where AI continues to evolve around us, our real point of difference, the thing that truly matters, will be our shared human connection. The warmth, care and understanding side of business – that's where we'll shine.

From the first spark of 'maybe I could do this myself', to the realities of making money, staying compliant, growing, employing and somehow managing to keep your sanity throughout it all, this book will be your guide and companion to help you accelerate your understanding and your business.

Why me?

Before you spend any more of your precious time and energy on this book, it's fair to ask, why me? I get it. I'd be asking the same thing! With more than 25 years across banking, construction, landscaping, and small business, everything in these pages is designed to be easy to read, easy to action and easy to come back to. It's shaped by real experiences working with real businesses who faced challenges and opportunities, and used their numbers, and the insight those numbers delivered, to bring incredible results.

I've used those experiences to create a book that can be your pocket guide to business; there when you need it, like a personal business advisor in your pocket!

How to use this book

And that takes me to our next point – how to use this book? As a pocket guide, this is a book you can dip into whenever a question pops up, so you can quickly get the information or guidance you need and move on with your day.

In light of that, you don't have to read it cover to cover (unless you want to of course!). I'll be honest, I'm not the strongest 'sit down and read a whole book' person either. I love listening on Spotify, flipping to the useful bits or finding exactly the section that speaks to what I'm dealing with right now. The only problem with this approach is that sometimes I miss the hidden gems – the little trade secrets or stories that touch my heart. And when it comes to your business and your numbers, it's those little things – the tiny little tricks of the trade – that can change everything.

So I've written this book with those treasures sprinkled throughout. Short, simple, powerful pieces you can find and use easily. So, simply pick what you need, and leave the rest. But carry it with you and continue to dip in and use it when another need arises.

My hope is that this book becomes a companion, a guide and a source of small, steady transformations that you can refer to again and again on your own business journey.

So, let's begin. Your business and peace of mind deserve it.

May you be all that you can. Be bold, be brilliant, be YOU... and let's *accelerate* together.

~ Keri

Accelerate your progress

This book comes with a little extra support along the way.

Start by scanning the QR code below to watch a short welcome video where I'll introduce the book, explain how to use it and share what I hope it helps you achieve in your business.

Then, throughout the chapters, you'll find more QR codes linking to short videos where I unpack key ideas in greater detail, walk through practical examples and discuss and unpack the chapter further for you. The goal is to help you move from simply reading the concepts to actually applying them with confidence.

Chapter 1

Why knowing your numbers changes everything

'What you don't know can hurt you.' – *Peter Drucker*

There's a quiet, unsettling moment that happens for a lot of business owners. It's usually late at night after your work day is done. The last email's been sent, you've managed your family or personal obligations and you finally have a moment to open your banking app or glance at the latest Profit and Loss statement. And suddenly you feel that terrible tightness in your chest.

You realise that things aren't really adding up.

Suddenly you're panicking. What if you're not making enough money? Have you covered all your costs and expenses? Will you be able to make payroll? Or, have you set aside enough (or any!)? Have you even thought about the ATO?

Feeling unsure about these things is a terrible, lonely feeling. But guess what – you're not the only one feeling it – and it doesn't mean that you're bad at business.

It's not that you're bad at business

In the course of my practice, I've met hundreds of business owners over the years, each with big dreams, brilliant ideas and a desire to make their dream come true. They've got all the right things in place – a great product or service, an amazing team, targeted marketing and more. Yet I've also seen time after time how challenging it can be for many of them to operate successful businesses that thrive and grow.

The reality is that it's not because these business owners weren't good at what they did. They just didn't know how to understand their numbers. And because they didn't understand their numbers, they weren't able to gain the insight they needed to make the moves that a successful business needs.

If you're feeling the same thing, you're probably in the same place. You may not really understand your numbers.

This uncertainty doesn't come from an inability to run a business, from laziness or lack of intelligence. It comes from not being taught how to understand the money side of business in a clear, practical way. And most of us weren't taught this... ever. Not at school. Not in life. And not by most of our bookkeepers or accountants. We learned how to work hard, but not read a Profit and Loss statement or plan to meet our tax requirements (and what are they anyway!).

But really, truly understanding them is the key to knowing whether you're doing OK, whether you'll make payroll and whether the time you're spending in your business is really worth it. So we have to learn these things if we want to truly succeed in our business. Here's why.

The real cost of not knowing your numbers

As business owners, if you don't understand your numbers there is real risk and a real cost. In Australia and New Zealand, the statistics are sobering. In Australia, 48% of all new business start-ups don't make it past the first four years, and around one in five don't even make it through their first year (the actual number is 23%).[1] The RBA also reports that since 2019-20 'more than half of new sole traders did not survive beyond three years'.[2] That's not because those individuals had terrible ideas – though some might have, of course – or didn't work hard enough. Instead, according to the Australian Banking Association, poor financial management sits alongside weak leadership and inadequate planning as one of the core reasons small businesses shut their doors.[3]

ASIC's insolvency data adds another layer for Australian business owners and shows that things aren't getting any easier. In the 2023-24 year alone, more than 11,000 Australian companies entered external administration, the highest number seen in over a decade.[4] The important point of this is that the majority of these businesses were small and medium-sized organisations.[5] Registered liquidators reported that poor financial control contributed to the failure of around 36% of companies entering external administration in 2023–24.[6]

1 Inside Small Business. (2022). 'Almost half of new businesses fail within their first four years.' Inside Small Business. Retrieved April 4, 2026 at https://insidesmallbusiness.com.au/latest-news/almost-half-of-new-businesses-fail-within-their-first-four-years.

2 Chan, P, Chinnery, A & Wallis, P. (2023). 'Recent Developments in Small Business Finance and Economic Conditions.' Reserve Bank of Australia. Retrieved April 4, 2026 at https://www.rba.gov.au/publications/bulletin/2023/sep/recent-developments-in-small-business-finance-and-economic-conditions.html.

3 Banks, L. (2018). 'New study reveals why Australian SMEs fail.' UniSA. Retrieved April 6, 2026 at https://www.unisa.edu.au/media-centre/Releases/2018/new-study-reveals-why-australian-smes-fail/.

4 Australian Securities and Investments Commission. (2024). Annual report 2023–24. Retrieved April 6, 2026 at https://download.asic.gov.au/media/nwridckz/asic-annual-report-2023-24_full.pdf.

5 Australian Securities and Investments Commission. (2024). Annual ASIC insolvency data reveals increase in companies failing. Retrieved April 6, 2026 at https://www.asic.gov.au/about-asic/news-centre/news-items/annual-asic-insolvency-data-reveals-increase-in-companies-failing/.

6 Bolivar, R. (2025). 'ASIC urges directors to protect small creditors.' *Insurance Business Magazine.* Retrieved April 10, 2026 at https://www.insurancebusinessmag.com/au/news/sme/asic-urges-directors-to-protect-small-creditors-535544.aspx.

And when you dig deeper, one theme keeps popping up – cash flow problems.

Chronic cash flow problems are widespread. Analysis of the data found that around 92% of Australian small businesses experienced at least one month of negative cash flow in 2021, with many facing the same problem several months each year.[7] And ASIC data shows that these cash flow problems are one of the main causes of company failure.[8] It's not sales. It's not effort. And it's definitely not a bad idea. Instead, it comes down to not having enough visibility over the money that's coming in and going out.

In New Zealand, the picture looks very similar. Cash flow is a persistent, systemic challenge for New Zealand small businesses, with poor cash-flow management and weak forecasting commonly seen in distressed and insolvent firms.[9] Further international evidence and policy analysis indicate that small firms are especially vulnerable in their first few years, and that weak financial literacy, poor financial management and cash-flow problems are major contributors to small-business failure.[10] Not great.

What's important to understand here is this – most businesses don't fail suddenly. Instead, they slowly run out of money. It might start with missing a tax bill they weren't prepared for. Or it could be that they're underpricing their work without even realising it. Or they might even be growing more quickly than they can actually afford.

---

7 King, P. (2022). 'Cash flow gap plagues 90% of SMEs.' *Accountants Daily*. Retrieved April 10, 2026 at https://www.accountantsdaily.com.au/business/17325-cashflow-gap-plagues-90-of-smes.

8 Australian Securities and Investments Commission. (2012). Insolvency statistics: External administrators' reports 1 July 2011–30 June 2012 (Report 297). Retrieved April 10, 2026 at https://download.asic.gov.au/media/2195190/rep297-published-7-september-2012.pdf.

9 Stride, N. (2022). 'Cash flow woes point to more insolvency in New Zealand.' CPA Australia. Retrieved April 10, 2026 at https://www.cpaaustralia.com.au/public-practice/inpractice/business-and-advisory/cash-flow-woes-more-insolvency-new-zealand.

10 OECD. (2020). Financing SMEs and entrepreneurs 2020: An OECD scoreboard. OECD Publishing; Busila, A. (2025). 'Thriving Through Seasonal Cash Flow Challenges: Strategies for Seasonal Small Businesses.' *Small Business Institute Journal*. Retrieved April 10, 2026 at https://sbij.scholasticahq.com/article/147327-thriving-through-seasonal-cash-flow-challenges-strategies-for-seasonal-small-businesses.

Whatever the precise reason, this comes down to not understanding their cash flow, and their overall numbers. And by the time this problem becomes evident, the damage has often already been done.

Xero's Australian research puts a very human face on this. In a recent report, they found that around one third of Australian small business owners said they couldn't pay themselves because of cash flow pressures. One third! The real number is in fact 34%, meaning 34% of business owners are making no income in their own businesses.[11] Instead, many had to dip into their personal savings accounts just to keep going.

Again, that's not poor effort – that's poor visibility.

When you don't know your numbers you're:

- Stuck in a mode of reaction
- The last one to get paid
- Pressured to make decisions based on fear rather than insight

And that's the real cost. It's the constant uncertainty that sits in your belly, keeps you up at night and quietly steals your confidence just when you need it most.

When the numbers start working for you

On the other hand, when you do know your numbers, awesome things start to happen. And the data shows that this isn't just feel-good fluff, but real, game-changing insight that makes a measurable difference for business owners across the board.

11 Xero. (2023). 'Aussie small business owners are forced to increase prices and dip into personal savings to combat cash flow woes.' [Media Release]. Retrieved April 10, 2026 at https://www.xero.com/au/media-releases/xero-study-reveals-small-business-cash-flow-woeso/.

Once you begin to understand your cash flow – for example, what's coming in, what's going out and when it's happening – you can start to predict and plan instead of just reacting. Experts report that businesses that actively examine their cash flow forecast at least annually are around 30% more likely to avoid financial distress than those that don't have the process in place to look ahead and get clarity on their liquidity and position.[12]

This matters because cash flow isn't just a technical term on a spreadsheet. In a very real way it's the difference between you being able to meet your next payroll, pay your tax on time (or at all), hire much needed staff or invest in the next phase of your business. When you understand it, you can make sure that you have enough money set aside for daily operations and unexpected costs without scrambling at the last minute – and without having to forgo paying yourself!

The thing is that when businesses engage with their numbers, they're far more likely to be able to take proactive steps that protect their business and support long-term continuity. Businesses that are able to survive cash flow uncertainty have owners that take steps like reviewing expenses, maintaining a cash reserve and adjusting their pricing to cope with the ups and downs of business ownership. Because knowing your numbers also puts you in a stronger position to make strategic decisions, not just survival decisions. And that means you're better placed to allocate your resources wisely, identify when it's safe to invest back into your business and recognise when you might need to tighten your belt (though with the help of this book, hopefully those moments will become fewer and farther between).

And there are more benefits that don't show up on your Balance Sheet, but matter just as much – including two of the most important,

12 Small Business Australia. (2025). 'Cash Flow Crisis: Why 80% of Aussie SMEs Are Struggling.' Retrieved March 16, 2026 at https://smallbusinessaustralia.org/cash-flow-crisis-why-80-of-aussie-smes-are-struggling/.

which are your confidence and your wellbeing. When you have a clear view over your cash flow, your margins and financial position, you'll feel more confident in your day-to-day conversations and decisions. You'll stop feeling dread every time you open your banking app or take a look at your financial reports. You won't change the subject every time anyone asks how work is going. And you won't be worried that there's something bad lurking just out of sight, because you'll know what your business is doing, and is capable of doing, every step of the way.

That confidence isn't visible to anyone else – not even to your bookkeeper. But it can certainly change the way you feel about your business in your day-to-day life.

In the same way, your wellbeing can be drastically affected when you feel good about your financial situation. There's a growing body of research showing just how much financial clarity and stress affect our overall mental health and quality of life. People experiencing financial stress are far more likely to report poor mental health and high levels of psychological distress compared with those who aren't under financial pressure.[13] In one ASIC-commissioned analysis, Australians facing financial strain were about twice as likely to also be experiencing mental health challenges[14], and an Australian Institute of Family Studies report found the men experiencing financial stress had a 53% increased risk of developing mental health conditions and even an increased risk of physical health conditions.[15]

---

13 Guan N et al. (2022). 'Financial stress and depression in adults: A systematic review.' *PLoS ONE*; Soomin, R & Fan, L. (2022). 'The Relationship Between Financial Worries and Psychological Distress Among U.S. Adults.' *Journal of Family and Economic Issues.*

14 ASIC. (2022). 'ASIC commissioned research confirms relationship between money and mental health.' Retrieved March 16, 2026 at https://www.asic.gov.au/about-asic/news-centre/news-items/asic-commissioned-research-confirms-relationship-between-money-and-mental-health/.

15 Woldegiorgis, M, Flood, M & Daraganova, G. (2025). Financial stress detrimental to men's mental and physical health – and vice versa [Media release]. Australian Institute of Family Studies. Retrieved March 16, 2026 at https://aifs.gov.au/media/financial-stress-detrimental-mens-mental-and-physical-health-and-vice-versa.

For small business owners in particular, the link between financial challenges and emotional wellbeing is very real – I've felt it, and I know you've felt it too. In a recent national survey of Australian small business owners, cash flow came up again and again as the biggest source of stress. Around four in ten said it had been a major factor affecting their mental health over the past year.[16]

Financial clarity won't magically remove every worry, but the research does show that when financial stress eases, the emotional load often eases too. In other words, your peace of mind increases, your underlying tension releases and you have the space to focus on running your business and enjoying your life – and that's the point, isn't it!

Understanding your numbers isn't just about keeping the lights on or your staff paid. It's also about understanding when and how you can grow, sustainably, without creating a rod for your own back or putting your business at risk of going under. This is the shift that matters – when you can move from guessing and reacting to understanding and choosing – then you can make decisions that boost your business, and your life.

Benefits of knowing your numbers

- Greater confidence in pricing your services or products because you understand your costs, margins and what you actually need to earn to remain profitable and competitive
- Fewer nasty surprises at tax time because you're setting aside money intentionally instead of just hoping for the best (and many of us do just hope for the best!)

---

16 Wilson, I. (2025). 'Australian SME owners report 'stable' mental wellbeing.' Accountants Daily. Retrieved April 16, 2026 at https://www.accountantsdaily.com.au/business/21398-australian-sme-owners-report-stable-mental-wellbeing.

- Improved cash flow stability, with a clearer picture of when money is coming in and when it's going out
- The ability to pay yourself (and not just your staff) properly and consistently, without guilt or fear
- More control over business decisions, which means that hiring, growth in general and even investment becomes a strategic choice rather than a reactive one
- You're able to initiate better long-term planning, with the confidence that lets you think beyond this month or even quarter
- You'll reduce your stress and mental load because you're no longer avoiding your numbers or worrying about what you might find, but using them give you vital information to support your business overall
- A business that supports your life rather than one that constantly demands more from you

These are not abstract benefits – they show up in how you sleep, how you plan and even how you talk about your business. They let you smile confidently whenever someone asks, 'So how's work going?'

A real example of what knowing your numbers can do

It's one thing to know the benefits of understanding your numbers in the abstract. It's entirely another to see them in action in real life. So let's explore that.

A few years ago a client came to me after being referred by another business owner we worked with. He was a sole trader, just starting out, but with big hopes and a very grounded outlook. From the beginning, he knew his goals and was very strategic about how to achieve them.

So what were those goals?

1. He wanted to put enough money aside to cover any tax payable.
2. He wanted to make a genuine profit.
3. He wanted to eventually employ his partner in the business to create a better work-life balance for their family.
4. And he had one more important goal (keep reading to find out!).

Our team often described him as a 'diamond in the rough'. He wasn't flashy or loud in his business decisions or work. But he was quietly committed to doing things properly, including getting ahead of his numbers and creating a sustainable business.

From day one, he made the decision to leave money in the business rather than take everything out for himself. In fact, we encouraged him to pay himself more on a few occasions, but he chose to forego this additional income and keep things modest in the beginning because he had his eye on something bigger – buying his first home.

We worked together consistently every month, reviewing his numbers, such as P&L, sales and cash in the bank. We talked through decisions, including bringing his partner on board and what the bank balance would need to be to cover her wages. We worked towards his goals by managing pressures and embracing opportunities as they came up, keeping an eye on his timelines and celebrating when he reached his milestones. There was no panic, no scrambling and no nasty surprises because he knew his numbers and understood where his business stood every step of the way.

Two-and-a-half years later, the results spoke for themselves. He'd paid all of his tax in full, every quarter, without exception. He brought his partner in, first on a part-time basis, then full time. He saved a solid house deposit (in fact, it was more generous than he'd even expected), and purchased his first home (the important goal we alluded to above!). Even better, he still had profit left over after lodging his tax return.

This wasn't an overnight success story. It was the result of a committed business owner who was willing to put in the work to understand his numbers and had the confidence to act on the insights that those numbers provided him. But the part I really want you to understand is that this isn't an outcome that happened because our diamond in the rough was naturally good at numbers. He wasn't. *But he was someone who was willing to listen, learn and engage with his numbers, and that willingness changed everything.*

Where this chapter leaves you

Here's what I want you to take away from this chapter. Knowing your numbers isn't about becoming a math whiz, or even a Xero expert. It's about giving yourself options – strategic options.

These are the kinds of options that let you plan ahead instead of scrambling when things go wrong. They help you understand where your business is actually at, so you can grow it with confidence and build something that supports your life, not something that slowly takes it over.

Right now you might feel unsure about your numbers and that's OK. That's why you're here. Awareness is the most important step, because now you know what you need to do, and we're here to do it together.

In the next chapter we'll start breaking this down into simple, practical pieces that give you understanding and insight. You don't have to worry about jargon or 'accountant' talk. I wouldn't do that to you! We'll just focus on the core building blocks you need to understand what's really going on in your business, and how to work with it, not against it.

Accelerate your progress

If you'd like to know more about the ideas we talk about in this chapter, scan the QR code below. It will take you to a short video where I expand on the key points of this chapter. This additional content is designed to help you start applying the ideas here with more confidence. Sometimes hearing it explained in a practical, real-world way is just the thing to make it click!

Chapter 2

Why we avoid our numbers

'Facts do not cease to exist because they are ignored.'
– Aldous Huxley

So now we understand why our numbers – and understanding our numbers – are important. You've seen the benefits of knowing them, and the cost when you don't. So now the question becomes – if we understand why it's important, why don't more business owners do it?

The reality is that despite their importance, research shows that many Australian small business owners simply don't use their numbers in a way that helps them grow and succeed in business. Many have low levels of financial literacy and, even worse, say that they 'rarely' use their financial reports for decision making.[17] And a national study of Australian small business owners also found that there are huge gaps in understanding around pricing, cash-flow

17 Isle, M & Freudenberg, B. (2021). 'A Comprehensive Analysis of the Business Literacies of Australian Small Businesses.' *Journal of Australian Taxation.*

managing and interpreting financial information as well.[18]

Why? Well, it's not because we don't care. Or because we're incapable of understanding. It's because there's a lot that gets in the way.

This chapter is about naming those barriers – the things that might hold you back from not only understanding your numbers but using that insight to accelerate your business for greater and greater success. And once we name those barriers, we can then learn how to move past them together.

Financial literacy

Many of the biggest barriers to understanding our numbers have nothing to do with effort or intelligence. Instead, they come from gaps in knowledge (through no fault of your own), a lack of confidence and experience or even because you just don't have enough time to get it all done on your own.

What's important to remember is that these are all incredibly common among business owners.

We were never taught this

For most business owners the first and biggest hurdle is simple – no one ever taught us how to understand our numbers. Of course, most of us *know* numbers. We were taught maths in school, so we know how to add, subtract, multiply and divide and most of us even understand more complex mathematics (like algebra, trigonometry and beyond). But very few of us were taught practical tools, and for

18 Brimble, M et al. (2025). 'Examining the financial and commercial literacy of Australian Indigenous small business owners.' *Accounting & Finance.*

business owners, this includes how to read a Profit and Loss statement, understand cash flow or know our break-even point.

Even if you can read your reports and statements, it's another step again to be able to read it in a way that gives you real insight into how your business is doing. But that's exactly what we need to be able to do.

This isn't a 'you' problem – it's a systemic gap. When terms like 'P&L,' 'GST,' 'PAYG,' 'Balance Sheet' or 'cash flow' come up, they can feel intimidating or confusing, especially when you have no real frame of reference. It's not that they're impossible to understand. It's because they're unfamiliar. But when you're running a business, this can lead to feelings of embarrassment or even shame. We think we *should* know this stuff – but really, there's no reason anyone should, unless they've been taught this. In other words, there's no reason that you should know this stuff. (But isn't it great that you're here to learn!)

I have a friend who is highly educated, with two degrees and a masters in law. She even practiced in the finance law space. If anyone should understand their numbers as a business owner, she thought it would be her. Yet, when she started her own business, she was surprised to find that she didn't really know what she was looking at when it came to her own financial statements.

It wasn't because she wasn't smart enough or educated enough, but because she just hadn't learned how. And this is a problem that many business owners share.

When something feels unfamiliar, we tend to avoid it. And this is true of our numbers as well. On the other hand, the more frequently people are exposed to something, the more comfortable they are and the more they prefer it over other options. This is known as the 'mere exposure effect', and for us it means that the more we work with our numbers, the easier it will become.[19]

---

19 Cherry, K. (2023). 'Mere Exposure Effect: How Familiarity Breeds Attraction.' Very Well Mind. Retrieved March 16, 2026 at https://www.verywellmind.com/mere-exposure-effect-7368184.

With the right exposure, experience, language and support, your numbers can start to feel understandable and manageable, and you can start to feel more empowered over time.

Fear of what we might find

Another one of the core blockers that keep business owners from diving into their numbers is the fear of what we might find. Sometimes we're afraid that things aren't as good as we hope. Sometimes we're afraid of discovering that we've made mistakes. And sometimes we're afraid that our numbers will confirm what we already suspect about our business.

So we delay. We put it off. We tell ourselves that we'll look later, when we have more time, or things get a bit more settled or (and this happens a lot) once that big invoice is paid. But the trouble with this is that avoiding the numbers doesn't fix anything. And it certainly won't make the stress go away. In fact, research shows that it usually makes it worse.

Experiential avoidance (this is where individuals are unwilling to engage with certain experiences) can even lead to mental disorders and post traumatic stress disorder.[20] That's because the unknown takes up more mental space than the truth ever does. And the longer we avoid looking, the heavier it can feel. So, while we might not find ourselves that deep in the mire with our financial statements, we can certainly find our stress levels, worries and anxieties worsening if we avoid our numbers.

20 Wang, Y, Tian, J & Yang, Q. (2024). 'Experiential Avoidance Process Model: A Review of the Mechanism for the Generation and Maintenance of Avoidance Behavior.' *Psychiatry and Clinical Psychopharmacology.*

We're time poor and overloaded

I'm a business owner, just like you, so I get it. Running a business is full on. It's not just about being good at what you do. It's also being able to juggle clients, staff, emails, admin, marketing, family and your life – and somewhere, in all of that, we're meant to find the time to work through our numbers as well.

We're time poor. We're overloaded. And we're tired. This makes it easy to let things that are perhaps important but not urgent – not *demanding* of our attention – slip to the bottom of the to-do list. This isn't because they don't matter. It's because other things are louder and push them down and out of mind. And this often happens to our numbers too.

Our numbers are always there, but they're often in the background, waiting for us to log in and check them out. They don't demand our attention (except maybe when the ATO gets involved!) and even when we do think about checking them out, we can sometimes be put off because we don't know how to do it easily. If we don't have simple systems in place, even small financial tasks can feel time-consuming and draining.

Between their lack of demands, and the fact that we don't know how to check them efficiently, we can easily ignore our numbers, and we often want to, because when time feels scarce, anything that feels hard is easy to push aside.

Too much tech, not enough clarity

I love technology. When it's done right and fits our needs it makes many things much easier. But in some cases, it can also create a false sense of security.

Accounting software, bookkeeping apps and now AI tools can give us a feeling that our numbers are 'being handled'. Sometimes we can assume that once we get all set up in Xero or, get our budgeting software running, that the system will just take care of the rest, or, at least, will let us know if there's a problem.

But the reality is that the tools only work as well as the data going in and the understanding behind them. There's an old saying in tech and finance that fits perfectly here – garbage in, garbage out. If the information going into your system is incomplete, inconsistent or incorrect, then what comes out the other side won't be reliable either – no matter how good the software is.

If the data going in isn't right, or if you don't know what the reports are actually telling you, then the output (when you get it!) can be confusing or even downright misleading. Instead of giving you insights, it blocks them. Instead of making things easier to understand, they look more confusing. And instead of helping you see your numbers clearly, the numbers look more complicated.

Tools are powerful. They can absolutely make your life easier. But they need humans – they need you – to interpret and manage them. Yes, even AI tools. Because at the end of the day, software can process information, but only you can interpret what it means for your business.

Bad data breaks trust

One of the fastest ways I've seen business owners disengage from their numbers is when they feel like they're wrong. Out-of-date reports, incorrectly coded transactions or months-old information can make the numbers feel irrelevant or unreliable. Or just plain wrong. And when you don't trust what you're looking at, then you stop looking at it altogether.

I've seen this happen many, many times, but one instance in particular has stuck with me. A client had been in business for a few years. She was working incredibly hard, but every time she logged into her accounting software or opened her reports, she felt a knot in her stomach. Her Profit and Loss just didn't match what she knew was happening inside her business. Some months showed losses when there had been lots of work (and lots of revenue). Other months looked surprisingly strong, but her bank balance told another story entirely. She couldn't make it work out, so eventually she stopped looking at her financial data altogether. She assumed the numbers were just 'accounting stuff' and figured she'd find out what was going on, probably at tax time.

When we finally dug into the issue together, we found that the issue wasn't her business at all. It was the data. Her transactions were being coded inconsistently, her income hadn't been reconciled properly and her expenses were sitting in the wrong place on the Balance Sheet. Once we went in and cleaned the data up, the picture suddenly came into focus. The numbers started to make sense and align with her experience in the business. The relief she felt was immediate, and her confidence came back almost overnight.

Bad data isn't usually intentional (or if it is, you might have bigger problems!), and it wasn't intentional for my client either. Usually what happens is that someone has fallen behind the data input, or you don't have the right processes in place, or no one has ever shown the person responsible in your business what 'good' data actually looks like. In many cases, it's because your business has grown faster than its systems, which just haven't been able to catch up.

Studies into financial reporting quality show that relevant, reliable and timely financial information is the foundation for better management and investment decisions. However, poor-quality information increases uncertainty and undermines your assessments of your business.[21] A global survey of more than 1,500 decision makers also reported that 46% of CFOs relied on 'gut feel and instinct' to make decisions, because they didn't have fast access to accurate internal data. Those same executives linked poor data to delayed decisions and costly mistakes.[22]

When you can't trust the information from your numbers, then it's almost impossible to make good decisions, and feel confident in making them. You need to learn to do it right or you could be making more trouble for yourself in the long run.

Reframing our blockers

If any of this sounds or feels familiar, it's time to take a big breath. None of these mean that you're failing, that you're not a good business person or that you're not intelligent or good enough. All they mean is that you're human and you're in the same position as so many other business owners.

The blockers are common and understandable (we've literally all had to deal with one or even all of these!). They don't say anything about your potential or your commitment. They simply describe where you're at right now.

And the great news is that they're also eminently solvable. Once you know what's been holding you back – whether it's time pressure, confusing systems or simply not being taught – you can

21 Cascino, S et al. (2016). 'Professional investors and the decision usefulness of financial reporting.' European Financial Reporting Advisory Group. Retrieved March 16, 2026 at https://www.efrag.org/sites/default/files/2023-11/Professional%20investors%20and%20the%20decision%20usefulness%20of%20financial%20reporting.pdf.

22 Epicor Software. (015). 'Head Or Heart? How do CFOs Make Decisions.' Industrial Distribution. Retrieved March 26, 2026 at https://www.inddist.com/operations/news/13767723/head-or-heart-how-do-cfos-make-decisions.

start to really understand your numbers and you can start to move forward.

Your goal isn't to become a numbers guru. You're probably not training to be an accountant. And there's certainly no exam at the end of this book. Your goal isn't perfection, but it *is* visibility and progress. You need enough understanding to know where you stand, what's coming and what choices you have, because it's this that leads to progress.

The 5 Pillars of Being in Business

When it comes to progress in your business, Karen Ashton-Bradley, who works with me in our business, and I noticed something important. People don't sit neatly at one point in their business forever, and nor should they. Instead, they can tend to progress through a series of stages, which we call The 5 Pillars of Being in Business.

5 PILLARS OF BEING IN BUSINESS

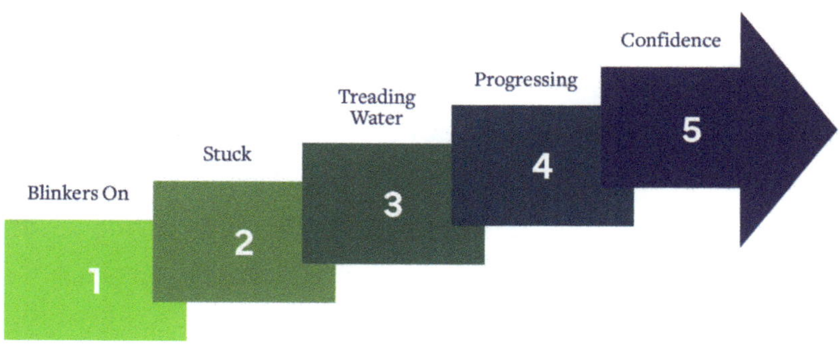

Pillar 1 – Blinkers on

This is where many business owners find themselves – at a point where you're just focused on doing the work and getting through the day. You're in survival mode, with blinkers on, hesitating to look around you. The business is operational and money is coming in, but there's very little visibility. Instead, the numbers feel distant, opaque or even uncomfortable, so you keep your head down and push on. You're just surviving, not necessarily because things are bad, but because looking feels overwhelming.

Pillar 2 – Stuck

At this stage, you know that something isn't right. The stress is getting more overwhelming and cash flow feels tight or lumpy. You feel like you're working harder than ever but not seeing any reward. The numbers are there, but they're confusing or confronting, and that can make you feel paralysed or stuck. You want to understand, you want clarity, but you don't know where to start or how to get there.

Pillar 3 – Treading water

At this stage, your business feels more stable. Your bills are getting paid, and so is your staff, and while the business is ongoing, your growth feels slow or uncertain. At this level, there's a lingering sense that there might be something you're missing, and that you could be doing better if you really understood what was going on beneath the surface.

Pillar 4 – Progressing

At this stage you're engaged with your numbers, and things are starting to change. You're reviewing reports, asking questions and making intentional decisions. Your confidence is growing and momentum follows. You still don't know everything, but you understand enough to plan and respond rather than react.

Pillar 5 – Confidence

At this stage, you're confident with your numbers. You know that they're correct and trustworthy. And you're also confident in your ability to gain insight from them. That doesn't mean that everything is perfect. But it does mean that you know where you stand in your business. You understand your cashflow, your margins, your break even point and your ongoing obligations. All of this means you can make decisions clearly, pay yourself properly and plan for the future well. Here the numbers are visible and supporting you instead of scaring or worrying you.

Your goal for the future

Your goal is to become a Pillar 5 business owner – running your business with confidence in your numbers and prepared for the future. But if you're not there, that's OK. There's no right pillar to be in right now.

Please don't use these as an opportunity to judge yourself. Instead use them to gauge where you are, so you can recognise your starting point, and the path you'll take to move forward. Once you can see where you're standing, then it's much easier to choose the next step.

The rest of this book is here to help you move along the path. In the next chapter we begin taking our first practical step together, by going back to basics and building a foundation that makes everything simple, calm and far more manageable. If you feel you already understand the basics (if you're already in pillar 3 or 4), you might feel ready to move onto some of the later chapters already. And if you're just starting out as a business owner, there's a chapter for you too.

Wherever you are, we're going to travel this road together, learning to understand the numbers, and gain insight from them, to take your business from success to success.

Accelerate your progress

If you'd like to go deeper into the themes we covered in this chapter, scan the QR code below. It will take you to a short video where I talk about it in more detail.

A small shift in how you think about your numbers can open the door to much bigger progress in your business.

Chapter 3

It's all in the basics

'The beginning is thought to be more than half of the whole.'
– Aristotle, Nicomachean Ethics

Whenever we learn anything new, we start with the basics. When we learn maths at school we start with counting, because you can't add and subtract, let alone tackle complex formulas, without basic numeracy. When we learn to read, we start with letters, because you can't read words, let alone sentences, without the alphabet.

These are foundational elements of learning. 1, 2, 3, 4, 5... A, B, C, D, E... and so on. And yet, when it comes to business, we often forget that the same principle applies. We get sent our financial statements, and when they don't make immediate sense we think, 'These are too complicated,' or, 'This is for the finance people.' But the truth is that your business numbers are built on the basics too.

In this chapter we're going to strip back and start from the beginning. If you think you don't need this, you might be right, and you should feel welcome to skip to the sections that you do need. But if you have the time, I suggest you give it a read anyway. It never hurts to strengthen the foundation. Because before you worry about the reports, fancy tools or even forecasting, you need to first understand what it actually costs to run your business. These are your basics.

Basics matter more than you think

Imagine you're setting out on a long road trip. You've got your snacks, a Stanley water bottle and your favourite audiobook ready to go. But before you set out you also need to know where you're going, how far you can travel before you need fuel and whether you've got enough money to get you there. You need a map – one that you understand.

Running a business is no different. Your numbers are your map. They tell you where you go, how you're going to get there and whether you've got enough 'fuel' (cash flow) to get there. And once you understand that, you can make informed choices about what you need to do next, which could be adjusting your pricing, slowing down hiring (or speeding it up) or finding a smarter way forward.

Unfortunately, a lot of business owners are on the road without a map and have no idea how far they can reasonably go before they end up stranded on the side of the road. These business owners are doing the work; they're busy, they're putting in the effort, but they don't have enough visibility to see how they're actually travelling and if they're actually going to get to their destination.

This metaphor might be a little overused – but I like it because just like a good map will help you get to your destination more quickly (because you know where you're going and the best way to get there), when you understand your numbers, you'll find success faster. You stop driving blind, stop making wrong turns and get to your destination that much quicker.

The basics give you the map because they give you a stable

foundation. They allow you to make informed decisions instead of emotional ones. And they help you understand whether growth is actually helping you or quietly hurting you (either financially or mentally!). Most importantly, understanding the basics gives you the confidence you need to move forward without constantly second-guessing yourself and the strength of your business.

This is real clarity (and yes, that word is also overused, but it's also true!). Complexity is the enemy of clarity, and when you understand your numbers, you get clarity, and lessen complexity.

And all of this starts with knowing one magic number in particular.

The magic number – your break-even point

Your break-even point is one of the most important numbers in your business. But it's also one of the most misunderstood.

So what is the 'break-even point'? Simply put, it's the amount of money your business needs to earn to cover its costs. That's it. Just costs. This isn't about making a profit, or paying yourself a bonus or even hiring new staff. This is literally the amount of money you need to keep your doors open.

This is your magic number.

When you understand what you need to keep your doors open, you also know what you need to invoice weekly, monthly or yearly just to stand still (that is, stay exactly where you are in the business). But now, you also understand something else – what you need to invoice in order to start making a profit, because that number is just over your break-even number. You also know that if you're below that number, you're going to slowly drain energy, cash or personal savings, often without even realising it.

Your break-even number is absolutely unique to your business. It doesn't matter what anyone else is making, earning or spending; that is relevant to their business alone. Instead, your magic number depends entirely on your overheads, your business structure, your pricing, your payroll costs and how you operate. There's no universal break-even point. There's only yours.

How to determine your magic number

While your number is unique, the break-even point formula is the same for everyone.

Fixed Costs ÷ (Price - Variable Costs) = Break-Even Point in Units

In order to solve this formula for your business, you need to know the following:

- **Your fixed costs** – the expenses that stay the same each month, no matter what you sell. Typically rent, insurance, software subscriptions, admin costs, etc.

- **Your selling price** – how much you charge for your product or service
- **Your variable costs** – the costs that increase the more you sell (for example, these could be materials or subcontractor fees)
- **Your expected sales volume** – how much you expect to sell over a given period of time

Once you have these figures, you can work out how many sales you need to make before your business starts covering its costs. When your sales number reaches your costs this is your magic number – the number you need to achieve each month to just break-even.

Watch your costs

However, it's important to understand that your break-even number isn't a 'set and forget' number. Your costs will change. Your rent might go up. Or your software subscriptions could creep higher. Insurance will continue to increase and wages as well. Your pricing needs to move with those costs or your margins will quietly shrink and you could be trading in a loss position before you know it.

This is one of the most common reasons business owners feel like they're working harder for less. Because if you don't watch your costs, then you really are. The solution here is to keep on top of your numbers. Review them regularly. It's not a sign that something is definitely going wrong, but it is the way you protect your business... and yourself.

Knowing your magic number changes everything

It might sound over the top, but knowing your break-even number truly can change everything in your business. It allows you to:

- price your services with confidence
- understand and ensure that a busy month is also a profitable one
- see the impact of rising costs before they become a crisis
- plan for growth without fear or panic

It also helps you understand whether the business is supporting your life, or taking more from you than it's really giving.

Knowing your magic number allows you to have confidence in your business. It doesn't mean that everything will be perfect. Sometimes your magic number might even allow you to identify when things are going wrong. But because you know where you stand, you can make the decisions you need to move your business forward in the right direction.

When you don't know your number

On the other hand, when you don't have any idea of what your break even point in business is, you can find yourself without confidence or insight into the best decision for you. I've worked with many business owners over the years and there's a clear difference between those who choose to understand their break-even point and those who don't.

Those who don't, work incredibly hard, but almost always feel uncertain. They might have good months and they might have bad months, but they don't really know why. So they end up reacting to what's happening instead of planning for it.

Not every dollar is yours

One of the most important things to understand as a business owner is that not every dollar is yours. We've already talked about how running a business is like going on a road trip. And that's very true. But being a business owner is also a lot like guarding a punnet of blueberries at a family picnic. There are lots of little hands and if you don't keep an eye on things those delicious blueberries will very quickly disappear. But the thing is that you do also have to share (after all it is a picnic).

Your business money is the same. You are entitled to it, but only some of it. Some of it you have to share – these are things like tax, expenses, subscriptions, super and more. And most of the time, these things want their share before you get yours.

For a business owner just starting out, it's easy to see every dollar as yours. You do the work, money comes in and you get to spend it. This is especially true when you're making less than $75,000 because it's only at this turnover stage that you need to register for GST. Until then, you don't have to register for GST, and if you're operating as a sole trader, it all simply feels like income. This can be a trap that's easy to fall into.

I have quite a few clients that are in the construction industry. Here's a common scenario. You've been an apprentice and you're earning say $45 to $50 an hour. Because you're an employee your tax is deducted automatically, WorkCover is taken care of and your employer pays your super. So the money that lands in your bank account is actually *your* money.

However, many apprentices, once they finish their training, turn to subcontracting. So rather than being employed by a business, you essentially become your own business. This is great as suddenly your pay rate jumps to $70 to $80 an hour, and that feels like a huge increase. But the thing that many people miss is that being paid $70 to $80 as a subcontractor is not the same as being paid $70 to $80 an hour as an employee.

Now that pay needs to cover your income tax (PAYG), superannuation, insurances, WorkCover, admin and compliance costs *plus* your own income.

What does that really look like?

Let's say your annual income sits around $100,000:

- First, you'll likely need to set aside around 30% for tax. That money doesn't belong to you. It belongs to the ATO.
- Second, you need to cover the costs of running a business. It's not unusual for these costs to take another 15% or more of your income. These are things like:
    - Superannuation
    - Insurances, such as Workcover, public liability or income protection
    - Fuel, vehicle costs, repairs, tools or other equipment
    - Work gear, uniforms and safety gear

When you add that together, around 45% of what you earn isn't yours. That $70 to $80 pay rate quickly becomes something much closer to what you were earning before – or sometimes even less – once you factor in what costs you're now responsible for.[23]

23 The ATO has great information that explains how to determine whether a worker should be legally treated as an employee or an independent contractor for tax and super purposes in Australia. You can find this information at https://www.ato.gov.au/businesses-and-organisations/hiring-and-paying-your-workers/employee-or-independent-contractor.

GST is helpful, but not free

Goods and services tax (GST), as we've seen, is another area that can trip up sole traders and new business owners. When you register for GST you're required to start collecting an extra 10% on behalf of the ATO. You can think of yourself or your business as a clearing house where you collect the GST, you offset it against the GST you have paid out of your business and the balance is payable back to the ATO. The money collected is not yours – it's simply passing through your business.

While you're not required to register before you reach the $75,000 threshold, registering early prior can be helpful if you have high start-up or operating costs, because you can claim back the GST on those expenses. For example, if you need to buy tools or equipment, vehicles or other large upfront purchases, it might be worth registering anyway.

But registration also comes with compliance requirements. You'll need to lodge BAS, keep records and be very disciplined with your cash flow. Whether or not it's the right move depends entirely on your situation, and it's something worth discussing with your accountant. There's just no one-size-fits-all answer.

When growth creates new problems

As your business grows, this concept – not every dollar is yours – becomes even more important. Once your turnover climbs into the $200,000 to $250,000 range, many sole traders start edging into the highest personal tax bracket. At that point it makes sense to look at whether a company structure is more appropriate for you. The reason this is a good idea is because profits can be taxed at a lower rate.

As an individual in the highest tax bracket, you might be paying

45% in tax, but your company profits will only be taxed at between 25% and 30% (based on 2025-26 year), which is much better. Again, understanding your numbers will give you the insight you need to make a good decision about your business structure as you grow. Always reach out to your accountant or business advisor to discuss this prior to making any changes. They will be able to work out what is right for you and help guide you through the transition from sole trader to a company or trust structure.

Where it all comes together

Once you understand that not every dollar in the bank is yours, the next step is learning how to see your business money as a system, not a single number.

Some business owners find themselves looking at their finances through just one lens at a time. Some focus almost entirely on revenue (in fact many!). These people think if I just work harder or sell more then everything will be fine. Others constantly watch cash flow, checking their bank balance and hoping it will be enough to get them through the next payroll or BAS. They've just got their fingers crossed. And quite a few others only think about compliance when a bill lands in their inbox with a thud.

But the problem is that you need to be thinking about revenue, cashflow and compliance together if you want the full story.

BUSINESS LENS MODEL

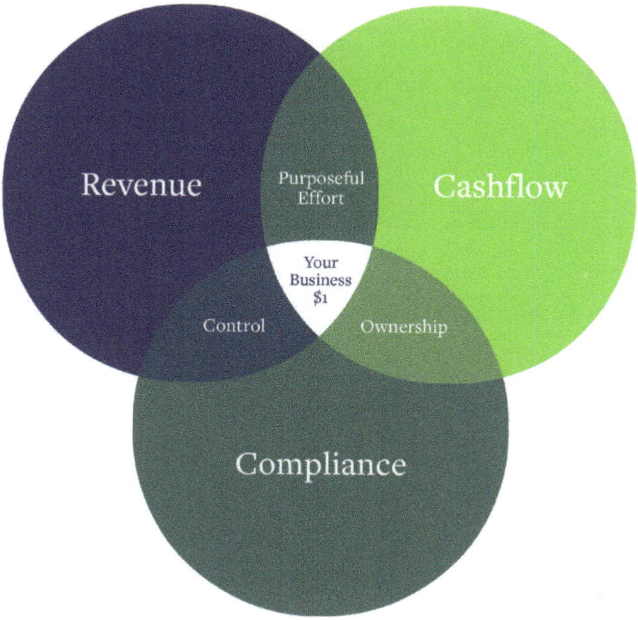

A healthy business sits at the intersection of revenue, cashflow and compliance.

- **Revenue** – money coming in. Most people think about revenue first, but on its own it can be misleading. You can be busy, even booked out, and still feel constantly under pressure if the other pieces aren't in place.
- **Cashflow** – timing matters. Cashflow is about when money comes in and goes out. It's the difference between being profitable on paper, and paying your bills in real life. This is important because most businesses don't fail because they weren't profitable, but because the timing of money simply didn't line up.

- **Compliance** – money that was never yours. Compliance is quiet, but can be hugely stressful. This includes tax, GST, super, PAYG and other obligations. This is money that might pass through your bank account but is never really yours.

At the intersections of each of these some great results pop out.

→ **Between revenue and cashflow you find purposeful effort** – because when you understand not just how much you're selling but when the money actually lands, you stop working blindly and start focusing your time and energy on work that genuinely moves the business forward.

→ **Between cashflow and compliance you find ownership** – because once you're deliberately setting aside what isn't yours and planning for obligations ahead of time, you move from reacting to bills to actively taking responsibility for your business finances.

→ **Between compliance and revenue you find control** – because when you price and sell with tax, super and other obligations in mind, you can make confident decisions knowing the business is structured to support you and compliance costs are accounted for and don't catch you out later.

Real insight comes through understanding revenue, cashflow and compliance together. This overlapping space is where your real business money is – that is, the money you can safely use, plan with and rely on. When you only focus on one circle, you're guessing. When you understand all three together, then you're finally in control.

Purposeful effort replaces busyness, ownership replaces avoidance and confidence starts to build.

With this lens in mind, it's time to start thinking about practical steps.

The steps to understanding your numbers

Understanding your numbers doesn't start with fancy reports, software or dashboards, but it does start with a few, simple practical steps that can help you see what's really going on underneath your business and can help you find your break-even number.

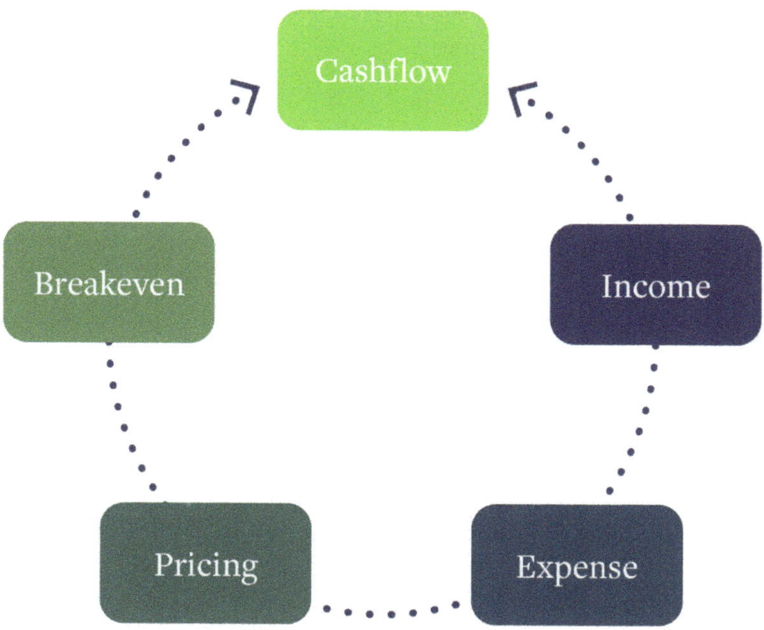

Step 1: Work out your costs to the business

At this stage we're only talking about costs to the business – not materials. So this means your general overheads (the fixed costs whether you're busy or quiet) and labour (the cost of people's time, including your own). This is especially important for service-based businesses, but it also applies to product-based businesses before we layer stock and materials back in.

Step 2: List your fixed overheads (monthly)

Rent, software, insurance, phone, bookkeeping, subscriptions – these are the costs you pay even if you don't have any revenue. Do this by referring to your P&L report for a six to 12-month period, then average those costs to set a monthly amount for each item. (Don't worry if this doesn't make perfect sense yet – we'll cover the P&L statement in Chapter 9 when we discuss financial reporting.)

Step 3: Add your variable costs

Next, add the costs attached to paying people. This includes wages, superannuation, contractor payments, payroll tax (if applicable) and WorkCover. These costs can shift depending on how busy you are, which is why it's important to include them separately rather than burying them inside your general overheads.

Step 4: Work out your 'actual cost to deliver'

Now calculate what it actually costs you to deliver your product or service each time you make a sale. This might include materials, contractor time, packaging, shipping, transaction fees, import costs or delivery time. In other words, this step is about identifying the direct cost attached to doing the work.

Step 5: Get clear on your pricing and capacity

Now move to the income side. What do you actually charge – your average sale, hourly rate or package price? And how many clients, sales or billable hours can you realistically manage in a month? Keep this realistic. This step isn't about what's possible in a perfect month but about what's sustainable in a normal one.

Step 6: Calculate your magic number

Now the fun begins. Once you understand your costs and your capacity, you can work out how much revenue your business needs to bring in each month just to cover its expenses. This is your break-even number – the point where the business is paying for itself, but not yet making a profit. This is what I call your magic number.

Step 7: Identify your profit margin

Now that you know your expenses and your magic number, you can choose what profit you want to make (with intention, not by accident).

You can set your target profit as either:

- a dollar amount, such as 'I want $2,000 profit per month', or
- a profit margin, such as 'I want to earn a 20% profit'.

From here you can calculate the revenue you need:

Revenue needed = expenses + target profit

Or if you're working from a margin percentage, use this formula:

Revenue needed = total expenses ÷ (1 – target profit margin)
(Tip here is to convert the % to a decimal-20% = 0.20)

Now you have two important numbers:

- the revenue you need to **break even**, and
- the revenue you need to **hit your profit goal**.

In other words, you now know: 'I need $X per month to break even, and $Y per month to hit my target.'

If you follow this process step by step, you'll have a much clearer picture of what your business needs to earn, not just to survive, but to succeed. Now you aren't just guessing – you're running your business with intention.

Building a foundation that actually holds up

By now you've done something many other business owners manage to avoid for years. You've slowed down and looked at the basics. The basics might be just that... basic. But they show you what it truly costs to run your business, what your break-even number is and why not every dollar in the bank is yours to spend. None of this is flashy, but it's all foundation. It's what your business is built on.

As the saying goes, 'In the middle of every difficulty lies opportunity.' For many business owners, the difficulty arises because they avoid looking at their numbers. The opportunity is what opens up once you finally understand them. Of course, this won't happen overnight, and you don't need to be perfect straight away. But it's important to get started, because once the foundation is in place, everything else becomes much easier.

In the next chapter, we're going to take this one step further. We'll look at how to make sure the information you're working with is actually reliable because even the best systems and tools can't help if the data going in is wrong.

Accelerate your progress

If this chapter helped you see the importance of the basics, the next step is seeing how they play out in real businesses.

Scan the QR code below to watch a short video where we discuss this chapter further to help you discover and find your break-even number and start using it to guide everyday decisions.

Chapter 4

Getting your data right (garbage in, garbage out)

'Data is a precious thing and will last longer than the systems themselves.' – Tim Berners-Lee, inventor of the World Wide Web

In this chapter we're going to focus on just one thing – making sure the information in your accounting system is actually correct.

One of the most common conversations I have with business owners always starts the same way. They sit down, open their reports and say, 'These numbers just don't feel right.' And they're usually correct.

I once worked with a client who felt they were paying too much to their staff. Whenever it came time for payroll, they felt that wages seemed to be eating a bigger and bigger portion of their revenue. They needed their workers to do their jobs – but they didn't see how they could afford to keep moving forward. They were seriously considering cutting back on staff hours but didn't see how they could then keep up with the workload.

So we started digging into their numbers. Much like my client that we met in Chapter 2, it turns out that it wasn't their cashflow that was the problem at all. It was the way the income had been recorded. Several large customer payments had been sitting in a suspense account rather than being properly allocated to sales. From an accounting perspective, it looked like revenue had dropped while wages stayed the same, making labour costs appear much higher than they really were.

Once we corrected the entries and allocated the payment properly, the picture changed. Revenue increased, labour costs returned to a normal percentage and the problem seemed to disappear. But nothing about the business had actually changed. The only thing that had changed was the accuracy of the data.

That's why getting your data right matters.

Garbage in, garbage out

As we've already mentioned, there's a well known saying in accounting and technology that applies perfectly here – garbage in, garbage out. Your accounting software doesn't think, question or interpret. It simply records what you put into it. So, if your transactions are coded incorrectly or inconsistently, or are left unreconciled, that's garbage in. And the reports that come out on the other end will be misleading at best and completely useless at worst – that's garbage out.

AI tools can exacerbate this because AI is still in its infancy. That means it can interpret data incorrectly. For example, it might code without GST where it's applicable, or misallocate it to accounts with similar names. These aren't a big deal in the short term, or as a one-off. (Hopefully it's something you verify and pick up on anyway!) But small mistakes can lead to bigger problems when it comes to insight. You can think of this like tightening the bolts on a bridge. Tiny slips might not matter in the short term, or in that specific instance, but they can lead to a total bridge failure in the future as they compound over time.

The same thing can happen with your business numbers. Small errors lead to misleading reports, even if the software (or the AI) is excellent. And when this happens – when the information you're getting out of your business just isn't right – then business owners start to disengage from their numbers.

When the numbers don't match reality, then your trust in them breaks down. And once you stop trusting your numbers, you just stop using them. That makes sense. Why would we rely on things that aren't true? So your reports sit unopened, decisions get delayed and your stress builds and builds in the background.

But the problem isn't you. It isn't the software. It isn't even AI. It's the data. We have to fix it so that you can trust your numbers again.

What is 'good' data?

Good data comes from correct data entry. And I know 'data entry' sounds confronting, but it doesn't have to be. Correct data entry doesn't mean everything has to be absolutely perfect, and it doesn't mean you need to understand the accounting rules inside and out. It means that you have a few simple, but critical, things happening consistently.

So what are these?

1. Transactions are entered regularly

The first thing is that you must enter your transactions regularly. Not months later, but soon enough so that you have good recall about what they really are, and have your bank balances to back you up.

2. Income and expenses coded to the right categories

Second, you need to make sure your income and expenses are coded correctly to the right categories so your reports really reflect what's going on.

3. Accounts are reconciled

Third, you need to make sure your accounts are reconciled regularly so your numbers reflect what's actually happening in your bank accounts.

At a minimum, this means checking that the bank balance in your accounting software matches your bank statement each month, or at least quarterly. It's a simple step, but it helps you catch anything the bank feed may have missed or duplicated before it becomes a bigger issue.

When those three things are in place then you can be confident that your data is good, and when you're confident your data is good, then your reports have a lot more meaning. But when they're not, they're pretty much meaningless.

Systems matter, but habits matter more

Before we talk about habits, it's worth acknowledging the role systems play. The right accounting software, bank feeds and basic automations remove a lot of manual work and reduce the chance of obvious errors.

A good system creates structure and sets the rules for how information should be captured.

This is also where a lot of business owners get caught out by modern automation. Bank feeds, software and AI tools can save you a lot of time. But they also make very confident mistakes. If you don't know what to look for, these small errors can spread quietly across your books and across the months.

We'll cover this in a lot more detail later in the book, of course, but for now, let's just keep in mind that good systems and tools make correct data entry easier, but alone they aren't enough. Good habits are actually what keeps things working. Regular reconciliation, consistent coding and routine review are far more powerful than complex setups that no one understands. Simple, repeatable processes create far better outcomes than complicated ones that are ignored.

This is absolutely supported by research. Habit research shows that repeated, consistent behaviour in the same context is what turns effortful actions into automatic habits.[24] Experts on habits also agree that setting a fixed schedule (for example, every Friday at 3pm I reconcile my bank feed) increases the likelihood that the task will actually happen.[25] Another way is to use structured checklists for routine finance tasks, which reduces errors and increases consistency and compliance.[26]

The goal isn't to create more work – it's to create reliability. But it's not always easy or straightforward. Habits help create that reliability!

---

24 Gollwitzer, P. (1999). 'Implementation Intentions. Strong Effects of Simple Plans.' *American Psychologist.*

25 Gollwitzer, P & Sheeran, P. (2006). 'Implementation Intentions and Goal Achievement: A Meta-analysis of Effects and Processes.' *Advances in Experimental Social Psychology.*

26 Manifestly. (n.d.). 'Boost Efficiency with a Daily Ops Checklist for Financial Services.' Retrieved March 17, 2026 at https://www.manifest.ly/use-cases/financial-services/daily-operations-checklist.

Common problems

When it comes to making sure you're getting good data out of your accounting systems, there are some common problems that I see every day. Most of the time, these data issues aren't caused by laziness or carelessness. They're usually the result of growth, time pressure or confusion about what to enter, or how.

Inconsistent coding

One of the most common of these problems is inconsistent coding. Typically this is when the same expense is recorded under different categories from month to month. The problem with this is that it makes it almost impossible to track trends, or understand where your money is really going, which is insight that can change how you run your business.

Missing or delayed data

Another issue that frequently pops up is missing or delayed data. These are transactions that are left unreconciled, invoices that aren't created or sent out on time or expenses that are forgotten altogether. Some of the most common gaps come from reimbursements, expenses paid for personally or costs that never went through the business account. These are easy to overlook, but they still form part of your true financial position.

Whatever is missing or delayed means that your reports might look complete on the surface but they aren't telling you the full story. And if they aren't telling you the full story, then they're useless.

Combining personal and business spending

Regularly mixing together business and personal expenses can cause some ongoing confusion. Your costs could be overstated or understated, your profit figures might be unreliable, you will have less visibility of whether you're absorbing personal expenses inside your business and you could lose the ability to see whether your business is performing well overall. Over time this blurs the line between what your business can genuinely afford and what it can't.

Accuracy creates confidence

When your data is accurate, something really great happens – you can start trusting your numbers again. That trust changes how you then use those numbers. Instead of avoiding reports, you refer to them for insight. Instead of reacting emotionally, or feeling rising stress, you're able to make calm, well-informed decisions based on patterns and facts.

Accurate data turns your accounting system from compliance obligation into a decision-making tool. It's what allows you to plan, adjust and grow without constantly second guessing yourself. Think about it like this. If you've been driving your car without a fuel gauge, you have no idea how far you can go, or even if you can get the car started. But now, you've fixed the fuel gauge, which means you have the information you need about whether or not you can go for a drive, or even a road trip.

It works the same with your business. Accurate reports give you the confidence to know how far you can go and grow with your business. That means you can answer questions like:

- Can I afford to hire someone, or do I need to wait another quarter?
- If you're a service based business, is this client actually profitable, or worth my time?

- Do I need to increase my prices because costs have crept up?
- Is this a quiet month, or is something genuinely off track with my business overall?

Accurate data turns your accounting system from a compliance obligation into a practical decision-making tool. You start to see problems earlier, not when they're already critical. You can spot opportunities in advance so you can decide whether they're right for you and your business. You can make decisions knowing what the business can actually support. And, most importantly, you get your sense of control back because you know where you stand.

Who's responsible for getting your data right?

This is a question that often comes up in my work, and it's a good one. Because someone does need to take the ultimate responsibility for making sure your data is right. But the answer isn't always straightforward – it's usually, 'it depends'.

If you have a bookkeeper, a BAS agent or an accountant supporting you, that's great, because those professionals are in the perfect position to support you and your business with the technical parts of keeping your data correct. But even with help, your responsibility doesn't completely disappear. You still need to make sure that the information being provided is on time and as accurate as possible. And working together, you and your support team will make sure that the transactions are entered and coded correctly, that they're being reviewed regularly and that the right questions are being asked when something doesn't look right.

In other words, even with help, this is shared responsibility. You absolutely don't need to do everything yourself (in fact, as a busy business owner, it makes sense to outsource these tasks to professionals). But you do need to understand enough to oversee the process.

How to make sure your data is good, not garbage

Here's how to keep your numbers clean and your data good. These steps assume you already have an accounting package in place, that you've set up your bank feeds and that you're willing to schedule a small amount of time to keep things current.

Step 1: Schedule a weekly review of your bank transactions.

Set aside time each week, ideally at the same day and time, to review your bank transactions. This doesn't have to be done by the business owner. It can be handled by a bookkeeper, team member or advisor, as long as it's clearly owned and done consistently.

During your review, work through a simple checklist:

1. Review each entry
2. Gather your receipts
3. Allocate transactions to the correct categories as you go

When you review your transactions close to when they happen, mistakes are easier to spot and your recall is much better.

Step 2: Schedule a weekly review of your financials.

Aim to review your financials weekly. You can do this at the same time as your bank transaction review, which often makes both easier, or at a separate time if that suits your schedule better. The key is to lock it in so it becomes a consistent habit.

If weekly feels like too much to begin with, move to a fortnightly rhythm. At a minimum, this should be done every two weeks so you stay close to what's happening in your business.

The aim here isn't a deep analysis, but familiarity. It helps to look at the numbers often enough so that you're able to start recognising what's normal for your business and what feels off.

Step 3: Schedule a monthly detailed review.

Your monthly review is where you slow down and look more closely at what's changed. This is the time to check that your income and expenses are all sitting in the correct categories, that nothing has been missed and that your reconciliations are complete.

A monthly review helps you catch small issues before they roll into bigger problems.

Step 4: Schedule a quarterly deep dive review.

Your quarterly deep dive review is where you set your business goals and access the information you need for your big picture thinking and overall business decision making. Quarterly reviews are important because they allow you to step back and look at trends over time, rather than reacting to what's happening week to week.

This also means you can move from just recording and reviewing to actively using your data to plan what comes next with your business.

This is also a good time to check in with your advisor or bookkeeper. Even a quick 10-15 minute conversation can help confirm that everything is on track, highlight anything you may have missed and give you confidence heading into the next quarter.

The steps in real life

One of my clients embraced this repeatable rhythm for real results in real life. He'd just been using spreadsheets to capture his financial data, and his first step was to move to MYOB. Then, instead of relying on a bookkeeper for everything, his team learned how to process and handle the initial steps themselves internally.

We still support them with their quarterly reviews so they have a safety net and someone experienced checking the bigger picture. But it means that their day-to-day bookkeeping and financial work is affordable and manageable. It turns out that for this client, it was a 'best of both worlds' approach – and with the steps above, you can take the same approach in your business as well if it suits.

Clean data means clear decisions

By now, you should be able to see that getting your data right isn't about being tech-savvy or 'good with numbers'. It's about creating the habits and systems that give you a solid base to work from. When your data is clean and consistent, your numbers start telling you what's really going on. They reflect what's actually happening in your business, rather than a muddled mix of personal spending, delayed entries or half-finished reconciliations. Instead, you're looking at information you can rely on, which makes decision-making steadier (and far less stressful!).

But accurate data on its own is only the foundation. The next step is learning how to read what that data is showing you without feeling overwhelmed or lost in accounting language. So, in the next chapter, we'll focus on a small set of simple, practical reports that every business owner should understand, not to satisfy compliance, but to answer real questions about performance, cash flow and sustainability.

Accelerate your progress

Getting your data right is the foundation for everything that follows. When your information is accurate, your reports start reflecting what's really happening in your business.

If you want to learn more about your data, scan the QR code below. You'll see a short video with more information about what you've just read in this chapter.

Chapter 5

Simple reports for stress-free finances

'Beware of little expenses; a small leak will sink a great ship.'
– Benjamin Franklin

Knowing what you owe at any time changes how you run your business – and I mean that quite literally. One of the most common things I see business owners doing is waiting. They're waiting for their BAS to be prepared. Waiting for an email to explain why their bank balance feels lighter than expected. And waiting for their accountant to tell them what's due, when it's due and even *what* to do.

It's always OK to rely on experts to support you in your business. Your bookkeeper and accountant can be an expert support in really understanding your financial position now, and forecasting for the future. But the problem with just waiting is that it puts you in a reactive position. And since you're the one running your business, you need to know what's going on. Otherwise you're making business decisions without visibility and just hoping that nothing unexpected turns up.

Reports are where your numbers stop feeling abstract and start becoming genuinely useful. When you have the right reports, and use them in the right way (and it doesn't have to be complicated), then you're in a position to use your financial information in a way that makes your business less stressful and your life much easier. And this chapter is about removing one of the biggest stressors for business owners – not knowing what you owe.

What we owe as business owners

Most business owners are on the hook for quite a few financial obligations, outside of the cost of running your business generally. These are things like GST, superannuation and PAYG ('pay-as-you-go' tax obligations). These concepts and the numbers behind them shouldn't feel mysterious – but they often do (and that's ok!). And they often feel like something only your bookkeeper or BAS agent really understands. If that's how you feel, you're in good company. Many business owners feel exactly the same way.

Reports are the simple way to gain visibility over what you owe. You don't have to replace your accountant, BAS agent or bookkeeper. But understanding where you are in your business allows you to stay in control. When you know where to find your GST, PAYG and super figures at any time, then you're no longer stuck running a business while feeling like your hands are tied.

Your business dashboard (a metaphor)

Think about running your business like driving a car. You don't need to know how everything works under the hood in order to be a confident driver behind the wheel. But you do need to understand your dashboard. You need to know what a fuel gauge means. You need to be able to recognise when a warning light comes on. And you need to know what speed you're travelling at (to make sure you're not going to get in trouble with the law!).

Your accounting system works in exactly the same way.

Once you know where to find the right reports, then you have access to your business 'dashboard'. You understand what the indicators are telling you. You can see how fast your business is moving, whether you have the capital to move forward and what the law (compliance) might need from you. In other words, you know what's going on. You've got all the information and now you can respond and take action, even if that means getting an expert on board to sort things out!

Knowing what you owe, when and to whom, gives you important business insight. And suddenly it feels like the ride is more controlled and far less stressful. You might even start to enjoy it a bit more.

Reports help you see

Here's the core of this chapter – you should be able to see your GST, PAYG and super obligations at any time, using the simple reports inside your accounting software. Most business owners don't have this information unless someone else tells them. And because of that, they assume it's complicated, technical or locked behind some complicated processes. But in reality, the information is already there

– on your dashboard – waiting for you to look at it. Of course, you have to know where to look.

When you can see this information for yourself, it gives you a lot of confidence. You know what's coming, you know what money is yours (and remember, not every dollar is yours) and you know where the rest of it belongs, whether that's back to the government in GST, paid out to the super accounts or set aside for your tax payments. Knowing that means you can plan properly instead of guessing.

Why this matters

You might be wondering why this matters. Why do you need to know how to find this information if you have an accountant or bookkeeper to tell you what's going on? Isn't that their job?

Yes, it is, and yes you're right. You can ask these experts to give you this information. But if you rely entirely on others to tell you what you owe you lose something important – flexibility and insight. That means that you might hesitate to make decisions. You might delay hiring, avoid investing or hold back on paying yourself because you're just not sure what's coming up.

This might sound funny coming from a registered BAS agent, and I'm 100% supportive of business owners having advisors. In fact, it's essential to outsource when you're growing so you can spend the time focusing on your own work and services. But empowerment – real financial empowerment – comes from understanding enough of your reports to verify, sense-check and be aware. When you know how to access these figures yourself, you're no longer in the dark between reporting periods. You're informed whenever you need to be. And when you're informed, you make better decisions.

In my work, I provide regular information and reports to my clients, and they trust the information I give them. Of course, I also back up every number with detailed ledger data as required. That works great and the clients get all the information they need. But the most confident clients are the ones who also know where and how to look this information up for themselves. They might not see everything in depth, but they know how to pull up a report and see whether things feel right – and they're also able to use the numbers to guide them when they need to make quick decisions.

This knowledge changes the relationship they have with their numbers. Those clients are engaged rather than dependent and that can make a huge difference to how they run their business.

The reports that matter

This chapter focuses on the most important, simple reports. And these can give you pretty much all the information you really need. You don't need a dashboard with 20 graphs. You just need a small set of reports that clearly show:

- **How much GST you've collected and claimed**, commonly shown in your GST Summary Report, GST Detail Report or GST section of the BAS report
- **What PAYG has been withheld or needs to be set aside**, commonly shown in your PAYG Withholding Summary, Payroll Liabilities Report or ATO Integrated Client Account Summary (which you can access via your agent or ATO Business portal)

- **What super obligations are building up**, usually shown in your Superannuation Payable Report, Super Liability Report or the super section of the Payroll Summary

These reports already exist in software like Xero, MYOB and QuickBooks Online. You don't need to create anything new. You just need to know where to go to generate the right reports. At the back of this book, you'll find a QR code which will take you to step-by-step templates and instructions showing you how to locate these reports in each system. Follow these instructions and you'll be able to generate the right reports whenever you need them, even if you've never done it before.

Remember, these figures will only be up-to-date if your bank transactions have been fully reconciled to-date. So keep that in mind, and maybe give it a quick check, as you generate these reports.

Compliance past, present and future

The interesting thing about compliance is that what's required hasn't really changed. Businesses have always needed to pay tax and super, and set aside GST. And they still do. But what has changed is how accessible the information is.

With modern software and better tools, there's no reason for these figures to feel hidden or intimidating anymore. They're easier to access than ever, especially once you know where to look. And with the coming AI initiates (some of which are already in place), it looks like things will become easier in the future.

Checking your financials can now become part of the routine of running your business, and can stop being a source of anxiety. And that's exactly how it should be.

Bringing it all together

This chapter builds directly on the work you've already done. You're learning about reports here, and how to access them, but the reports only work for your business because clean, consistent data (chapter 4) makes them reliable. You only have the context to what you're seeing because you know your break-even point (chapter 3). And you're only looking at your reports because you know why they matter (chapter 2). Together, these pieces allow you to clearly separate business money from money that was never really yours in the first place.

And knowing what you owe gives you more understanding and control... and therefore confidence in your business. Because when you stop being surprised by your obligations and start planning for them, that alone removes a huge amount of background stress from running your business.

Of course, even when your compliance numbers are clear, there's still another piece that determines how you feel about your business. For example, you might feel profitable and compliant – like you're doing everything right – and still feel like you're scrambling from one payment to the next. And that typically comes down to cashflow.

So that's where we're going to focus in the next chapter – on cashflow, the real lifeblood of your business.

Chapter 6

Cashflow, the lifeblood of your business

'Profit is secondary. Cash flow matters most.' – *Peter Drucker*

Peter Drucker is right – cashflow does matter most. In fact, it's the lifeblood of your business. When you have good understanding and control of the cashflow in your business, it's like having good circulation in your body. Good circulation means your blood is flowing and steady, your organs function well, your brain gets the oxygen you need and you feel good.

It's the same in your business. When cashflow is on point, not only is your business more supported, overall, but each discrete piece (or organ) is as well – from payroll, to hiring decisions, to when and where to scale. Even better, you can sleep at night.

But when cashflow is tight, everything feels so much harder. There's more pressure, it's harder to make decisions, especially time-sensitive decisions, and your business stops being any fun. You can find yourself operating in survival mode.

Understanding your cashflow, and embracing its insights to guide your business decisions, can make all the difference.

Cashflow is **not** profit

When it comes to cashflow, there's one thing we need to talk about first – and that's the idea that cashflow is not profit.

If this immediately resonates with you, you're likely in the minority. Because one of the biggest misconceptions I see in business owners is thinking that profit and cashflow are the same thing. But they are not.

In fact, you can be profitable on paper and still run out of cash. That's because profit is an accounting concept. It's numbers on a report. But cashflow is your reality. Cashflow is the net amount of cash (and cash equivalents) that move in and out of your business accounts over a specific period of time. So, you might have a huge month providing services, and invoice $130,000, but if no one pays those invoices during the month, you won't have any cash actually coming into the business.

Cashflow is essentially about timing. It's when the money actually lands in your account, and then moves out again, and that timing impacts whether you can pay your bills as they fall due, meet payroll and simply fund your business itself.

In simple terms, profit is whether your business model works, but cashflow is whether or not your business survives month to month.

Positive cashflow versus negative cashflow

Before we go any further, it's important to understand the difference between positive and negative cashflow because these are terms you might hear from your financial advisors or just in the world. So what are they?

Positive cashflow is where you have more money coming into your business than is going out over a given period. Negative cashflow means the opposite – it's where more money is leaving your business than is coming in.

Obviously we want positive cashflow. This is a great place to be because it means you have room to breathe and move in your business. You're not moving money around to cover payroll or costs and you're not relying on overdrafts or credit cards.

Negative cashflow looks different. You're delaying payments just to stay afloat, juggling bills and constantly trying to plug gaps. It's not a very nice place to be.

The benefits of strong, positive cashflow

When your cashflow is healthy:

- You can pay bills on time.
- You meet payroll comfortably.
- You reduce stress.
- You stop dreading the end of the month, or tax time.
- You can implement better personal financial strategies for yourself.
- You build confidence and credibility because your suppliers trust you, your banks trust you and your team trusts you.
- Most importantly, you trust yourself.

Consequences of poor, negative cashflow

When your cashflow is not healthy:

- You can't pay your bills when they fall due.
- Your bank balance doesn't bounce back quickly.
- The end of the month is stressful.
- You have to juggle money and accounts, or avoid or delay meeting your obligations.
- You can't grow or scale your business.
- Your energy drains away.
- Others may lose trust in you.
- You lose confidence in your business and yourself.

Why your cashflow matters

Research consistently shows that poor cashflow management is one of the leading causes of small business insolvency.[27] Industry inquiries and SME surveys repeatedly identify cashflow weakness as a major driver of small-business failure, alongside factors such as under-capitalisation and poor planning.[28]

In Australia, ASIC's external administrators' reports regularly identify 'inadequate cash flow or high cash use' among the top three causes of company failure, cited in roughly 45–50% of insolvency cases in recent reporting periods.[29]

27 Jirsch Sutherland. (n.d.). 'Poor cash flow cited as the leading cause of business insolvency.' Retrieved February 16, 2026 from https://www.jirschsutherland.com.au/latest-news/poor-cash-flow-cited-leading-cause-business-insolvency/.

28 Sakalouski, A. (2026). 'Cash flow pressures keep insolvency risks high – what SMEs should know.' ScotPac Business Finance. Retrieved 16 February 2026 at https://www.scotpac.com.au/blog/cash-flow-pressures-keep-insolvency-risks-high-what-smes-should-know/.

29 Australian Securities and Investments Commission. (2016). *Insolvency statistics: External administrators' reports (July 2015 to June 2016)* (Report REP 507). Australian Securities and Investments Commission; Australian Securities and Investments Commission. (2019). *Insolvency statistics: External administrators' reports (July 2018 to June 2019)* (Report REP 645). Australian Securities and Investments Commission.

At the end of the day, the success or failure of your business isn't always about earning more – and certainly it's not about working harder. Usually, it's just about managing better.

How to create positive cashflow

Having good cashflow allows you to run your business. It reduces pressure on you and gives you options on how to spend your money and grow your business. It allows you to pay your bills as they fall due, and lets you make decisions from a point of strength, instead of fear.

And when it comes to how to create positive cashflow, it starts with understanding your debtors and creditors.

Debtor and creditor control

If cashflow is the lifeblood of your business, debtor and creditor control is what keeps it moving.

Debtors, also known as Accounts Receivable (AR), represent the money owed to your business. Creditors, or Accounts Payable (AP), represent the money your business owes to others. Your AR and AP ledgers are the arteries and veins that control the movement of this lifeblood. That's because this is where you track what's coming in and what's going out.

When you deal with trading terms – and most businesses do – you will be affected by cashflow at some point. It's inevitable. Just as we discussed above, you might invoice today, but not be paid in quite some time. Or you receive a bill today, and you pay it later. It's between these two movements that sits your cashflow reality.

So, controlling the space between your debts and your credits is important to keeping your cashflow moving. Your ledgers are the tools that show you exactly what is happening in that space. They tell you who owes you money, how much they owe and what the terms are. And they do the same for those you owe money to.

The terms of these agreements really matter as well. If your debtor terms are 'pretty loose', you'll feel it. Customers will stretch payments. 30 days becomes 45. 45 becomes 60. And suddenly your cash is funding someone else's business. At the same time, if your suppliers are strict – for example, '30 days end of month' terms – you have a clear outgoing commitment.

Your business is unique, so how you manage your ledgers depends on your unique needs for your business as well. You might be tempted to simply shorten your terms with your customers and extend them with your suppliers. That would keep money coming in more quickly than it's going out. This is a really smart move. But you also need to remember that it's a balancing act. If you lean too far that way, you could damage your relationships with suppliers or customers. And if you lean too far the other way then your bank balance can feel this strain.

You'll have to consider what kind of terms your clients or customers will find acceptable. Is a seven-day payment period OK, or do those who engage someone in your industry expect 30 days? Do your suppliers expect payment on delivery? And if so, how often are you ordering, and how does this impact your cashflow during those periods?

These are the questions you have to answer – and the answers will guide how you manage your own debtors and creditors. You have to do so, because when your debtors' ledger reduces, your bank balance increases. And while this sounds obvious, many business owners tolerate high debtor balances believing that it's just part of doing business. This doesn't have to be the case, and it shouldn't be.

Stock considerations

Stock is money. If your business sells products, or otherwise holds stock, you need to think about how much you have, and how often it's turning over. For example, if your stock is just sitting on your shelves then it's simply not working for you.

So what can you do to turn your stock into cashflow? Use it intentionally and strategically.

But how do you use your stock intentionally and strategically?

Well, this will be different for every business, but a great place to start is to look at your stock turnover rate. How quickly does each product move? Are some items selling weekly while others haven't moved in six months? Do you know how long your cash is tied up in inventory before it comes back into your bank account?

If something isn't moving, you need to figure out why. Is it priced incorrectly? Is it being sold in the wrong location? Does it need to be sold or bundled with another product?

Once you figure out why it's not moving, you're halfway to a solution. You can bundle it with the right product, if that's the problem. You can discount it if it's not priced correctly – or simply lower the price altogether. You can sell it online or in person if one isn't working.

Sometimes business owners fall into the trap of holding onto slow stock because they've already paid for it and don't want to lose money. But sometimes selling stock that's just sitting on shelves can be the right decision, even if you're only making a small margin, or just breaking even. This might be a more strategic choice than leaving thousands of dollars tied up on shelves.

A real-life example – turning cashflow around

A few years ago, I worked with a client that had $100,000 in outstanding invoices owed to the business and $120,000 in bills he needed to pay. His accounts payable had terms of 30 days with an end of month due date, but the payment terms he offered his customers were much looser.

The business was busy, and on paper it looked like it was doing pretty well. But cashflow was misaligned and so our client felt constant pressure.

When I started working with this client regularly, the first thing we tackled were the outstanding invoices. Within 30 days, we reduced the $100,000 owed to the business to $70,000. It was a great start, but it wasn't enough. The next step was to review slow-moving stock. What could they sell or move, and how?

Within a few more weeks, money owed to the business came down to $50,000, which was a more acceptable level for his business. They'd identified their slow-moving stock and were able to move a good portion of that too. With that stock sold, cash, which had previously been tied up in inventory, was released back into the business, increasing the bank and strengthening their overall position.

Before the bank balance for this business fluctuated between $25,000 and $40,000. After tightening debtor control and freeing up their stock, their balance sits closer to around $140,00 to $180,000 per month.

Now, that's a great number, and the client felt a huge amount of relief when he could look at the accounts and see that money there. But even better, bills were being paid on time, the pressure was reduced on the owner and he could even start salary sacrificing for his retirement.

The important part to recognise is that nothing actually changed in the business itself. The client had similar revenue as he'd had in the past, and he hadn't suddenly acquired a lot of new customers or expanded into a new market. The only real change was improved cashflow. And that's the power of managing your AR and AP properly.

Practical steps to improve your cashflow

Improving your cashflow isn't complicated, but it does take focus and discipline. Here are some practical steps you can take today.

1. Be honest and realistic about where you're at.

You can't fix what you can't face. Look at your current debtor balance, and then look at your creditor balance. Then step back and look at the patterns or trends in these numbers over the past year or two. (You can ask your bookkeeper to help if you need!) Don't guess, or approximate. Really get to know the numbers. This is the only way to start making real improvements on your cashflow.

2. Bring your books up to date

Outdated books lead to outdated insights, and outdated insights lead to distorted decision making. Even if your data is only three months out of date, you lose important information that can guide how you run your business. So, bring your books up to date and then keep them there. Up-to-date books means up-to-date decisions.

3. Review your AR and AP ledgers

We've talked about this pretty deeply, but it's an important step in understanding your cashflow and bringing it under control. Review your creditors and debtors to find out who owes you money, how long it's been outstanding and if there are any patterns that can give you insight. And you will also need to find out who you owe information to, when those bills are due and if you're consistently pushing those payments out.

4. Chase slow payers

This is sometimes hard for many business owners, but you can chase slow payers in a way that is professional and even kind. You can send out reminders quite easily through most accounting systems. You can offer payment plans if needed. And you can restructure future work to include deposits or progress payments so you're not carrying a full cash burden upfront. The important thing is to get the process started because you can't control cashflow without *cash*.

5. Consider other payment options

Depending on your industry, you might want to consider offering alternative payment options such as Stripe, Apple Pay, Afterpay or PayPal. Some of these also allow you to offer instalment plans.

Having alternative payment options gives your customers other options for paying you 'on time', particularly if they're struggling themselves. And it can reduce the friction on your relationships too. The goal here isn't to encourage debt, but to remove barriers to payment for your customers, while also speeding up your own cash receipts.

6. Pay your bills before the due date

This often sounds counterintuitive to my clients, but paying at least some bills early can reduce the end-of-month pressure or the emotional dip that comes from watching your bank balance drop sharply before it rises again. If you space out your payments (rather than paying everything at the end of the month) you can control the rhythm and create predictability in your business.

7. Revisit your customer trading terms and enforce them

Check your customer terms. Are they working for you? If not, how should you adjust them? Once you have this set, remember that they aren't suggestions. They're agreements. If you set the terms at 14 days, then follow up at 14 days, consistently. When you enforce your terms calmly and professionally, your clients feel that as well, and are usually happy to adjust.

8. Review your slow moving stock

Don't hold onto your inventory if you don't have to. Stock is money. It ties up your cashflow, so if it's not moving, then it's not helping. If you're struggling to move any category of stock, think about how you can get it moving. Discount it, bundle it or offer it in some other way – but the goal is to clear it so you can turn it back into cash.

Cashflow and mental load

Before we move on from cashflow, I want to talk about one other side to the issue – and that's the psychological side. When your cashflow is unstable, your nervous system can be impacted. Research on financial scarcity and behavioural decision-making shows that financial uncertainty narrows your available mental bandwidth, which takes away from your ability to manage complex tasks or take on long-term planning.[30] Financial stress is also a form of psychosocial stress that can increase the stress hormone cortisol, and this is linked to impaired learning, increased anxiety and even trigger 'risk aversion' changing how you approach financial decisions.[31]

On the other hand, when your cashflow is stable it reduces your mental load, and that lets your thinking expand. You have mental space to plan and innovate. You're able to lead your business better, consider growth opportunities and just live a better balanced life overall.

Bringing it together

Cashflow isn't the most glamorous subject. It's a part of business that gets mentioned a lot behind closed doors, but rarely gets talked about at networking events. But it's fundamental. It's how you control and grow your business. Because when you improve your cashflow, you improve your options, which then improves your business, which then improves your life.

Never take your eyes off it.

30 Feinberg, C. (2015). 'Harvard's Sendhil Mullainathan on behavior and poverty.' *Harvard Magazine*. Retrieved March 18, 2026 at https://www.harvardmagazine.com/social-sciences/the-science-of-scarcity.

31 University of Cambridge. (2014). *Stress hormones in financial traders may trigger "risk aversion" and contribute to market crises*. Retrieved March 18, 2026 at https://www.cam.ac.uk/research/news/stress-hormones-in-financial-traders-may-trigger-risk-aversion-and-contribute-to-market-crises.

Accelerate your business

If this chapter helped you understand how cashflow really works, the next step is seeing it in action.

Scan the QR code below and access a video where I discuss this chapter in more detail for you, including how small changes can make a big difference to your day-to-day reality.

Chapter 7

Choosing the right tools

'Remember that time is money.' – *Benjamin Franklin*

There was a time when a spreadsheet and a shoebox of receipts was good enough for keeping track of your numbers. But if you want to run your business efficiently today, and have confidence about your numbers and the insights they give you, then you need a lot more than just a place to record your data. You need a system that helps you understand it. And software helps you do that.

When you utilise a software package everything is in one place – your income, expenses, payroll, GST and reports. And it's not just in one place, but it's also all connected. That means that you're not left trying to piece together information from multiple sources or waiting until the end of the quarter to see how things are tracking. You can see what's happening in real time, usually with one click of a report-generating button.

It also makes it easier to collaborate with your advisory team. You can share data with your bookkeeper, BAS agent and accountant – even better, they can access it directly. You don't have to send documents or information, and no one is working off of outdated information. And it's easy to bring on a team to help if you haven't yet.

In our practice, we provide regular monthly or quarterly compliance reports within agreed timelines. That works really well. But when our clients can log in whenever they need and access those figures themselves, something shifts for them. They're no longer passive recipients of information. Instead, they're engaged in their business and empowered to make decisions quickly and when it matters. And that's why it matters for you as well.

Work is going to fill up a large part of your life – so the systems supporting that work should help you do it well. The right software won't just record your transactions. It will give you speed, transparency and insight. And that's what allows you to move your business forward with confidence.

So when it comes to choosing your accounting software, the question isn't which one is the 'best' in general. The important question is, which one is the right tool for you? Just like you wouldn't pick up a butter knife to carve something intricate or use a sledgehammer to hang a picture frame, you need the right tool for the task at hand.

Your software options

As a BAS agent, I'm very often tasked with recommending a software package to my clients. It's one of the first questions new clients raise, and one of the most common conversations I have even with established business owners who don't feel they're getting enough out of their current system.

When it comes to making a recommendation, the reality is that systems are systems. Each of the major platforms – Xero, MYOB, Quickbooks – will record your transactions, generate reports and give you the information you need to stay compliant. So, any of these are a good choice – but none of them are a single 'perfect' system. You just need to find the one that works best for you in your business.

If you're working with an advisor and they recommend a particular platform, it's usually worth listening to their advice. They know how the system works. They know what you need. And they know how to support you best within that system. When your advisor is confident in and efficient working with a particular software, that efficiency also flows through your business.

Looking past the dollar

Cost matters of course because every business works within a budget. But when it comes to choosing your accounting software, it's a good idea to take some time to think beyond just price. A subscription fee might look slightly higher on paper, but the bigger picture is important. If a package is easier for your agent or bookkeeper to use, they'll be able to complete your work more efficiently. This reduces your outsourcing costs.

If you're doing the work yourself, the package that you can use easiest and most intuitively will also save you time. And when it comes to your own business, time is money of course. But reducing friction also means you'll spend more time in the software, getting more valuable insights about your business overall.

So, what appears more expensive upfront, might actually be more affordable or perhaps valuable overall when you factor in time, efficiency and insights.

My recommendation

I've been using MYOB for over 25 years, and I've worked with both Xero and Quickbooks since they first came to the market. I'm equally comfortable across all three, and continue to support clients in all three as well.

But if you ask me my personal preference, it's Xero. Why is that? Because it's incredibly easy to use. This software is intuitive and streamlined, which means we (or you) can complete your data processing more efficiently. This gives us more time to review your file properly, check in with you and provide meaningful support rather than spending your time on getting through the transactional processing.

In my experience, the other software options simply take more time for data entry. It doesn't mean they don't work, because they absolutely do. It just means the workflow is often slightly slower. And in our industry, time is literally money.

Ultimately, however, this is just one advisor's opinion. Your advisor will help you choose the right system to support your business, your budget and your team in the most effective way possible.

The steps for choosing your software for yourself

1. Understand the pros and cons

Every package has strengths and trade-offs. None are perfect. So the first step is to consider the benefits of each package, as well as its limitations. Your goal isn't to find the perfect package, but to find the one that's most suitable for you and your business.

2. Look at how the pricing is structured

How many users will need access? Are the features tiered? Is payroll included, or is it an add-on? Understanding how the subscription is structured will help you determine what its real cost will be.

3. Identify your priorities

One of your more important questions is to ask yourself what you really want from your accounting software. Is strong payroll functionality essential? Do you need inventory tracking? Are integrations with other apps important? When you're clear on what matters most, it will help you compare the right things between software options.

4. Consider ease of use

If you're entering data yourself (or even if you're just accessing it), your system needs to feel intuitive, and it needs to support efficient workflows. The less friction there is, the more time you save. And, as we've already mentioned, time is money.

5. Take advantage of discounts and trial periods

Most platforms offer introductory pricing or free trials. Use this time wisely. Log in, explore the dashboards and see how it feels to navigate through. Sometimes hands-on experience tells you more than any brochure or pros and cons list can.

6. Get others' experiences

Ask others for their experiences. Talk to fellow business owners and colleagues in your industry. Real-world experiences can offer valuable insights into what works and what doesn't.

7. Speak with your advisor

Your BAS agent, bookkeeper or accountant works in these systems every day. They understand your compliance requirements, reporting needs and workflows. They know what you need to build in efficiencies, to give you visibility and to save you money in the long run. Take their advice seriously – it's based on experience, not marketing.

8. Do what's right for you

At the end of the day, this is your business. So ask lots of questions and take your time in deciding. You need to choose the system that feels right and supports how you operate your unique business.

The right tool changes everything

This chapter isn't designed to tell you the software you have to choose. But hopefully it has shown you that your accounting software isn't just about compliance, or data entry. It's not just for ticking the BAS box or making sure you're lodging it on time. Instead, it's about having visibility, feeling in control and having the information you need, when you need it.

You can absolutely run your business without an accounting system. A lot of people do. But it's also a lot harder, and slower, and you'll find that you're stuck chasing numbers instead of using them for your benefit. And when you have your financial story all in one place, it can absolutely change how you show up as a business owner.

For you to be able to do great work, you need a great accounting package to give you the numbers you need. So choose thoughtfully and strategically, and then use it well.

Chapter 8

Systems and processes for operational excellence

'If you can't describe what you are doing as a process, you don't know what you're doing.'
– W. Edwards Deming

As a BAS agent, I spend a lot of time inside businesses, mainly looking at numbers. But those numbers don't exist on their own. They're the result of what's happening day to day. This is how work flows, how information moves and how consistently tasks are completed. When those processes aren't working this impacts your entire business, including your finances.

A few years ago I worked with a company helping them to systemise their financial processes. To get started, I sat down with each stakeholder to map how information moved through the business, starting from the moment a customer made an enquiry online, in person or over the phone. We looked to see what happened next, where the information went and who was responsible at each step.

What we found was that even though there were only four people in the office, the workflow was completely jumbled. The information jumped between the four of them multiple times, and instead of things flowing logically from enquiry to pricing to quoting to purchase order to supply to invoicing, it bounced around. Sometimes one person would handle one part, sometimes another. Paperwork was shuffled between, questions repeated and tasks interrupted. Everyone was waiting on someone else, and no one seemed to have ownership of anything to ensure it kept moving forward.

Everyone was working hard. They were engaged and competent. Nothing was 'technically' wrong – but nothing was working well, because it wasn't efficient. It took us six weeks of investigation and review, but ultimately we streamlined the process so that the work flowed in and through the business in a much more structured way. And this had fantastic results.

The staff were able to be more productive, which meant they could deal with more enquiries. More enquires meant more sales through the business, and that meant more revenue overall. Importantly, each person felt less friction in their day-to-day work – there was less back and forth, less questions between people and a lot less paperwork shuffling.

Every business needs good bones

My client didn't change anything major. It was the same team. They had the same workload. But now they had a better structure and much better results. That's the power of implementing good systems.

No matter how small your business is, you need processes and policies in place. You can think of this like having good bones. They don't necessarily make anyone pretty (they're on the inside after all!), but they make your body solid and functional. They support everything else – your muscles, organs and even skin. And they allow it to stand tall, move and even grow.

Processes are the bones of your business. When your workflows are documented, people know what needs to be done. Information and data flow smoothly, everyone knows what is going to happen and when, and, importantly, who's responsible for it. And this means your business can function consistently and repeatedly.

Most importantly, this allows your business to function with or without you. In Chapter 11 we'll cover this in a lot more detail, but it's important to recognise that you want your business to work without you because this means you can actually step away occasionally – and that's vital for maintaining a good work-life balance. Without documented processes, your downtime won't really be downtime. You'll always be the bottleneck, so you'll always have to be on call.

Tools to support your business

In my business, we use ClickUp. We've recently upgraded to a newer version which allows us to utilise it even more efficiently and deeply. For us, this system works really well. It saves us time, it creates repeatable processes and it allows us to document them too. We use it for recurring tasks, which we then assign to staff members. We also document our Quality Management System within it so we can make sure we're doing excellent work at all times.

Of course, this isn't an ad for ClickUp, and ClickUp is certainly not the only option for creating repeatable processes and systems in your business. There are other great tools – for example, Asana or Karbon. And there are new AI-supported options coming online all the time, such as Notion. Some business owners even prefer to document their processes in Word or Excel, and that's fine too. The tool isn't the most important part – it only matters that you're actually documenting the process, so find a tool that works best for you in your business.

Get your people on board

Once you've created and documented your processes, the next step is to make sure that your team or people within your business are using it, and using it properly. That's the only way to get any value out of any system. Because no matter how good it is, it's reliant on discipline.

You need to make sure that everyone on your team knows how to use the tools you put into place. This means giving them both training, and time to experiment with navigating through the system. Many systems have their own online training modules, and YouTube is another great place to access information. You can also speak to other people in your industry who use the tool to find out how they use it to get the most out of it.

Once you have your team on board, you don't have to document everything yourself. Part of the process can be teaching someone else how to do this for you or outsourcing to an expert. There may even be AI tools that can assist with capturing and organising workflows.

The key isn't perfection – it's just getting started, and then continuing to move forward together with your team.

How to start building your processes

If you try to fix everything at once, you'll overwhelm yourself. Don't do it! Just start small and then build momentum as you go along.

Here are some steps to get started, without the overwhelm:

Step 1: Create a safe space for open communication

If you have staff, involve them in creating and documenting their processes and systems. They're on the ground, and can offer valuable insight. Ask them what's working, and what isn't. Where things are challenging, work with them to identify where the friction sits.

Step 2: Write down 10 things that could be improved based on those conversations

Here are five questions to get you started.

1. What part of your workflow currently takes the most time or feels unnecessarily difficult?
2. If you could remove, simplify or automate one task in your role, what would it be and why?
3. Where do you see delays or frustrations happening in our processes?
4. What tools, systems or information would make your job easier or help you work more efficiently?
5. If you were designing our workflow from scratch, what would you change?

As a Manager/Owner, also think about removing yourself from this process so that your team/employees are happy to build this list together.

Once you've received this information you now have a broad view of what areas of your business need improvement, what can be systemised and what changes need to happen.

Step 3: Decide what you want to tackle first

Don't try to fix everything, or even create processes for everything, all at once. Be realistic with your priorities. What are two things that will make the biggest difference to your business? Ask your team to identify what they think, and then together create the priorities

From the five questions above my personal choice would be to tackle numbers two and four first. Why? Because question two just asks you to tackle one task, and it's easy to review, identify the issue and implement the solution. I'd also choose question four because it will make such a difference in your overall financial visibility. So, when your team members come back with their suggestion about which tool would be best, look into it. Do a cost analysis and if it's feasible implement it.

If it's not, then communicate that to your team explaining why. Ask them to focus on another item from the list that you could implement and explain why. Keeping open communication with your team is important.

Step 4: Test and refine

Once you've created and documented the process, use it. Get your team to use it in the real world, with their real work. And then adjust it as needed. Check in regularly with your team and ask them how things could be improved. If it's doable, appoint someone to be accountable for this process, or set it up as part of the workflow where they can put notes that can be reviewed regularly. If there are any areas that aren't working well, refine those further to build in more efficiencies and so that continual improvements occur.

Step 5: Move to the next priority

Once you have this process working smoothly, you can move onto the next one. Then start again with the steps. Be sure to complete each process properly, including testing and refining, before moving on.

Making the time

It's not always easy for business owners to find the time to build out their processes and systems. You may need to do this work in your downtime, or take some time away from your chargeable work. But this is an investment in your business's future, and your future efficiency. And small improvements to your processes can make big improvements in your business.

Accelerate your business

If this chapter helped you see how systems and processes shape your business, the next step is seeing how to build them in a practical way.

Scan the QR code below, where we discuss this chapter further – including how workflows are mapped and how improving them can help your business run more smoothly, with the results reflected in your numbers.

Chapter 9

The importance of financial reporting

'You can't drive a car if you're looking in the rear-view mirror. You have to look forward.' – Mary Barra, CEO of General Motors

You likely already have access to all your financial reports. But if you're like many business owners, you don't feel very confident reading them. We touched on this earlier in the book, and you already understand why your numbers matter. This chapter is about taking the next step – accessing your reports and understanding what they're telling you.

The key financial reports you'll be working with include your Balance Sheet, Profit and Loss, cashflow, budgets, forecasts and break-even analysis.

Each one of your financial reports gives you a different perspective on your business.

- Your Trial Balance checks that everything is lining up behind the scenes.

- Your Balance Sheet shows your position.
- Your Profit and Loss shows your performance.
- Your Cashflow Statement shows timing and liquidity.
- Your break-even analysis tells you your magic number.
- Your budgets and forecasts show you where you're heading and what needs to happen to get there.

Individually each of these gives you a piece of the information – but together, they give you a full picture. When you understand how these pieces relate to one another, your business stops feeling like a collection of transactions and starts feeling like a system. I often describe financial reporting as a jigsaw puzzle. When all the pieces are there and put into place correctly, the picture becomes clear. You can see the full image and the disparate pieces start to make sense. On the other hand, when pieces are missing, misplaced or misunderstood, you don't get the full picture of what your business truly looks like. You're trying to interpret something incomplete.

In this chapter we'll walk through each report in simple terms – what it shows, why it matters, how it connects to the others and what it helps you understand about your business as a whole. At the end of this chapter I don't want you to just be generating reports. I want you to understand what they're telling you.

Your financial reports

Knowing why something sits in your reports is an integral part of running a strong business.

Why is something in your Balance Sheet and not Profit and Loss? What exactly is a Trial Balance report? How do budgets, forecasts and cashflow fit together? And how does it all connect?

Your reports aren't separate documents floating around in your software. They're interconnected parts of one financial story. So, let's walk through them properly.

Trial Balance

Your Trial Balance report doesn't get as much attention as it should – but it does play an important role in understanding your financial position. You can think of this as your accuracy test.

The Trial Balance report lists all the accounts that feed into your Balance Sheet and P&L in one place. In a properly maintained system, your debits equal your credits. When they do, your books are balanced and ready for accurate reporting. So this report confirms that your underlying data is sound before you rely on it for the P&L or Balance Sheet.

If your data is wrong at this level, every report built from it will be misleading. So it's important to get it right!

Balance Sheet

You can think of your Balance Sheet as your business' snapshot at a single point in time. It shows:

- **What you own – your assets.** This includes your cash holdings, equipment, vehicles, stock and other tangible resources. They represent the overall value your business has.
- **What you owe – your liabilities.** This includes your credit cards, loans, outstanding debts and even tax obligations like GST and PAYG. These are your real commitments that need to be paid.

- **What's left – your equity.** Equity is the difference between your assets and liabilities. It represents the portion of the business that belongs to you once your obligations are accounted for.

Your Balance Sheet answers the important question, *where do I stand right now?* It shows you your current position, but it doesn't give you insight into how your business is performing as this comes from your P&L statement (your Profit & Loss statement).

Profit and Loss

The Profit and Loss statement, often just called your P&L, tells a different story – it tells the story of performance.

What does that mean? P&L tracks all your income and expenses over a specific period, whether that's weekly, monthly or yearly. In fact, you can generate reports for all kinds of time periods, including custom periods, though we typically focus on monthly or quarterly.

When you track it over a period of time, you can see whether or not you made a profit or a loss over that period. Income comes in. Expenses go out. And what's left is either profit, if you're in the black, or it's loss, if you're in the red. So if your Balance Sheet is your business's snapshot, your P&L is your movie over time. It answers the question, *is my business actually making money?*

This is the report most business owners look at first. It shows trends in sales, tracks costs and highlights where profit is being gained or lost. When you review it, it helps you understand how efficiently your business is operating.

But performance on paper, doesn't always equal cash in the bank. And that's where your next report comes in.

Cashflow Statement

We've discussed cashflow in depth in Chapter 6. So you already know how important it is to understand your cashflow overall. Your Cashflow Statement is your reality check because it answers the question, *can I meet my obligations right now?*

Understanding what cash is coming into your business and what's going out at any point means that you can easily recognise if you can meet payroll and pay your suppliers or contractors. Because the fact is that you can be profitable on paper and still short on cash. That's not uncommon at all. Your P&L may show strong sales, you might be busy every day, but if your customers haven't paid, or you have high obligations outstanding, your bank balance won't reflect that position. The Cashflow Statement highlights that timing and lets you know whether you can cover your upcoming commitments.

When you take the time to review your Cashflow Statement, one of the best results it brings you is reduced stress. It removes surprises and allows you to plan for the future.

Break-even analysis

We already know that your break-even number is your magic number. And it's also your financial checkpoint because it's the exact level of sales required to cover all your costs. Your break-even analysis lets you check in to make sure that you're working above the point where your business breaks even.

When you have a break-even analysis that you review and understand, you know:

- How much you need to sell to keep the lights on.
- Whether your pricing structure supports your cost structure.

- What growth actually needs to look like.
- How much buffer you really have.

Your break-even analysis shows you your magic number and whether your business is moving beyond it.

Budgets

Your budget is essentially your financial plan. It sets out what you expect your income and expenses to look like over a certain period of time. In your budget you will set targets and boundaries to give yourself financial accountability.

A budget allows you to compare what actually happened against what you forecasted. And that comparison is powerful because it's not just information. It's information that allows you to stay on track and make adjustments when and where needed.

Without a budget, there's nothing to measure your performance against. And that leaves you reacting to what happens rather than guiding the business overall.

Forecasts

Forecasts are a bit like budgets... but they take things a step further. While a budget sets expectations at the beginning of a period, before you take any real-life financial actions, a forecast looks ahead to help you understand what you can expect based on current data and trends. In other words, it uses what's happening now to predict what might happen next.

Forecasting can help you anticipate:

- Cash shortfalls
- Seasonal dips
- Growth opportunities
- Investment timing
- Hiring and supply needs

When used at their best, forecasts help you shift from reviewing the past to steering the future.

Bringing it all together

Each of these reports has its own purpose:

- **The Trial Balance** ensures your data's accuracy.
- **The Balance Sheet** shows your financial position.
- **The P&L** shows your performance.
- **The Cashflow Statement** shows your liquidity.
- **The break-even analysis** shows your survival point.
- Your **budgets** set your plan.
- And your **forecasts** guide your direction.

Individually, they provide insight. But together, they form the complete story of your business – where you stand, how you're performing and where to steer next. This is also where tools can make the process even more powerful. While all major accounting software options offer the financial reports you need, there are tools that can make drilling down into the details of the reports even easier.

For example, I use Spotlight Reporting alongside Xero for some of our clients. It imports data monthly and allows us to focus on specific areas – costs, sales, labour or whatever the client wants deeper visibility into. Spotlight Reporting presents the information visually, plotting trends and graphs so that patterns are easy to see... and therefore, easy to take action on. Clients can choose what they want to focus on and even how they want the information displayed.

If this kind of tool might be helpful in your business, speak to your advisor. They can help you find the right tool, assist you with the setup or set it up themselves to send you reports directly.

Of course, while tools are very helpful in segmenting out information, they can't take the place of real understanding. (Which is where this book comes in!) But they're excellent add-ons that create high-resolution insight into your financial health.

Practical steps

If you're ready to get started with your own financial reporting, here's how:

1. Start by ensuring your bookkeeping software is clean and up to date. Remember – garbage in means garbage out!
2. If you want deeper insight, consider linking your accounting software to a reporting tool (such as Spotlight Reporting). To do this, you'll need to decide what matters most to you – sales, margins, labour, overheads or cash movement – and customise your reports to deliver the information you need.
3. Work in collaboration with your advisor – or get an advisor on board if you don't already have one. You don't have to do this

alone. A financial advisor can help you with the setup and even manage the reporting process for you. The right support makes the process and insight far simpler.

When your reports are complete and accurate, your jigsaw puzzle suddenly fits together. The big picture becomes visible and that means you can make stronger decisions. That's the real power of understanding your financial reports.

Knowledge creates momentum

Knowing your financial reports is crucial for business owners to make informed decisions, manage risks and drive growth. When you understand your reports, you can stop guessing and start truly understanding your numbers. You can stop making decisions based on what your bank account 'feels like' this week. Instead, you can start making choices and decisions based on your real financial insight. That's not just reporting – that's real control and real decision making power. And better decisions are what ultimately accelerate your business.

Chapter 10

Making time for what matters

'Yesterday is gone. Tomorrow has not yet come. We have only today. Let us begin.' – Mother Teresa

A few years ago I met with a business owner who felt like time was slipping through her fingers. And because of that, she felt like her life was as well. She worked from dawn until well after dinner, and she still didn't feel like she was making any progress.

Her days were full. She had a packed schedule and emails flooding her inbox every day. She found herself answering calls between school drop-offs, replying to emails late at night and squeezing in her 'real' bookkeeping work 'where she could'. But despite all that effort she was stuck.

Every week felt like getting on a carousel and never being able to get off. It all looked the same. Round and round she went; busy, reactive and exhausted.

When we started working together I asked her what her top three priorities were for the business that quarter. She paused. I thought she was just taking some time to think, but in fact, she didn't have any idea. She hadn't been able to step back enough to ask where it was all going.

And that's when it became clear to her – she didn't have a time problem, but she did have a priority problem.

My job is as a BAS agent, advisor and bookkeeper, but I'm also a business owner. And I know from experience that running a business can feel like sitting in a taxi with the meter running. Every minute costs money. Every delay adds up. And you can't just ignore it because you know the number is climbing.

Productivity in your business matters. You need to be able to get your work done, be responsive to your clients, provide good customer service and actually earn money. But without structure, urgency will always overpower importance.

That's exactly what my client was experiencing. The phone would ring and she would answer it. An email would come in and she would respond immediately. The squeaky wheel clients and 'urgent' issues would demand her attention, and she would comply. And all these meant that she was working hard, but not necessarily on the things that moved her business forward.

Being time poor isn't always about having too much to do. Often, it's just about doing too much of the wrong thing at the wrong time.

In this chapter, we're going to look at how to take control back of your day, your tasks and your life. We'll touch on how to prioritise properly and how to create space – not just for productivity, but for your life outside the business too. Because time is money, but it isn't *just* money. It's also energy, focus and freedom, and you deserve more of that!

What happens when urgency runs your business

When urgency runs your business, everything feels important. That's because urgency is loud; it demands attention and it also creates the illusion of productivity. But it's not *real* productivity. At the end of an 'urgent' day (as opposed to a 'productive' day), you'll find you've been busy from start to finish, but the work that will actually move your business forward is still untouched. You won't have been able to spend time on strategic planning, reviewing your numbers, building systems or developing your team. Because these tasks don't shout in the same way as 'urgent' tasks, they're pushed to tomorrow, and then tomorrow again.

You might also find that you start to struggle with decision fatigue. Constantly reacting to what comes at you drains your mental energy, so instead of making deliberate choices, you start making quick ones, relying on shortcuts and default options rather than deliberation that takes real effort.[32] And these can often cost more in the long run.

When you constantly feel pressed for time, the pressure builds. You carry work into the evening, you sacrifice your breaks and you tell yourself that once things 'calm down' you'll be able to do the important things that are still sitting on your to-do list. But if you don't prioritise those things, they rarely ever do calm down enough.

This pressure will almost inevitably cause your stress levels to increase. And when you feel behind every day, these feelings of stress can actually become your default setting, leading to chronic stress.[33]

---

32 Polman, E & Vohs, K. (2016). 'Decision Fatigue, Choosing for Others, and Self-Construal,' *Social Psychological and Personality Science.*

33 Denovan, A., Dagnall, N., Drinkwater, K. & Escolà-Gascón, Á. (2023). 'Evaluating the psychometric properties of the Chronic Time Pressure Inventory using Rasch analysis.' *PeerJ.*

Financially, the impact is just as real. When you spend your high-value hours on low-value tasks, your profitability can quietly slip down the scale. Every minute has a dollar value attached to it, whether you've calculated it or not. That doesn't mean that we spend all our time working, but we do have to spend some time doing the work that brings in revenue or we won't have a business for very long.

But perhaps the biggest consequence of letting urgency run your business is that you lose control. And that's not because you're incapable or lazy, but because you're allowing external demands dictate your internal action.

Taking back control of your time

Making time for what matters doesn't actually mean working less. It means working deliberately. And that means identifying what truly drives your business forward, making sure you have the space for those tasks and letting go of the noise that doesn't.

The first step is simple. But it requires honesty – from yourself and to yourself – about what your real priorities are.

These aren't just the things that feel urgent (or are urgent). And they aren't the things that other people are pushing for you to do. These are the things that will actually move your business forward financially, strategically and operationally.

How to find your business priorities

To find your real business priorities, ask yourself, *what are the top five things that will genuinely drive my business forward this month?*

Write down those top five items, then focus on completing them one by one. But once they're done, you don't just stop. Instead, you turn to the next five, identifying those and completing them. Keep this cycle moving, continuing to focus and review.

Don't sweat the small stuff

When it comes to finding the work that will move the needle forward on your business, it's important to remember not to sweat the small stuff. That doesn't mean ignoring the details or lowering your standards. But it does mean learning to see the difference between what truly matters and what might just feel irritating at the time.

You know better than anyone what your weaknesses and strengths are. Maybe you overthink small decisions, or get distracted by minor issues, or spend too much time perfecting tasks that only require 'good enough'. If you focus on these things too much, they can start to consume more attention than they deserve. So, focus on the things you can change, not the things that you can't, and protect your mental bandwidth for the decisions and tasks that actually impact your business.

Minimise duplicative or low-value tasks

One of the biggest hidden drains on time is duplication. Answering the same type of email repeatedly, recreating documents from scratch, searching for information that should be easy to find when you have good systems or having to constantly switch between tasks due to interruptions.

Each of these things is small on its own, but can compound over time.

Instead of getting bogged down by these kinds of repetitive tasks, start by identifying them. Then consider what solutions might be available. Can you template them? Automate them? Systemise them? Maybe you could even build an AI agent to help take care of some of them.

Email is a good example, and it's one of the biggest time thieves in most businesses. If your inbox is open all day, and you're in it and replying, you're effectively allowing other people to set your agenda. Instead, set specific times when you'll drop into your inbox and reply to and action emails. This creates clear blocks in your day where you focus on priority work without your emails on.

When you reduce duplication and reactive habits, you increase your productive capacity without working longer hours.

Delegate

If you have a team, or work with contractors, delegation isn't optional – it's essential. You simply can't grow a business, or avoid burnout, if you try to do everything yourself.

But delegation isn't about offloading the work you don't like (though sometimes this works too). It is about allocating tasks to the people with the right strengths to work on them. When you're deciding if and what to delegate, start by asking, *is this something only I can do?* If the answer is no, it might be time to share the load.

However, delegation also requires structure. You have to have a system for passing on the work and building in accountability. You also have to set expectations and define outcomes. This includes setting deadlines and expecting them to be met.

Setting limits

In your work, it's important to set limits on things that might otherwise suck up your time. Client meetings should have clear start and end times, as should your team meetings. If your meeting is scheduled for 30 minutes, aim to finish it in 30 minutes. Without boundaries, conversations expand, agendas drift and the day disappears in small increments.

The same applies to availability. If you respond instantly to every call or email, that becomes the expectation. Instead, set clear communication windows and stick to them. Let clients and team members know when you're available and what turnaround times look like.

Limits aren't about being inflexible (and they certainly aren't about poor customer service!). But they are about protecting your focus. When you create boundaries, you stop urgency from dictating your schedule and start managing your time with intention.

Take breaks

You will have heard this many times, but it's important for you to have time out for you. This is the part that many business owners often resist because taking time for you feels 'lazy' or 'undisciplined'. But time out is not laziness – it's maintenance.

Research consistently shows that sustained productivity requires rest. Studies from Stanford University have found that productivity per hour declines sharply when a person works more than 50 hours per week, and drops off significantly beyond 55 hours. Beyond a certain point, more hours do not equal more output – they equal diminishing returns.[34]

---

34 Roberts, E. (n.d.). 'The relationship between hours worked and productivity.' Stanford University, Department of Computer Science. Retrieved April 24, 2026 at https://cs.stanford.edu/people/eroberts/cs181/projects/crunchmode/econ-hours-productivity.html.

Breaks actually improve focus, decision making and problem solving. Even short mental pauses during the day can increase overall efficiency. So scheduling time off alongside time on isn't indulgent – it's actually strategic. If you never step away, your thinking narrows. But when you create space, your perspective returns.[35]

Remember, this is a work in progress

Making time for what matters in your business is a work in progress for everyone. It's not something you can perfect once, and never revisit. It takes trial and error. Some weeks will feel smooth, but others will feel chaotic (even heavily chaotic). But that's OK, because our goals are not to attain perfection but to become aware and make adjustments where we can to continually build in more time for what matters.

In my own business, for example, I used to rely on handwritten to do lists. But as my business grew, this was no longer enough. Over time I adopted systems, in my case, ClickUp. This allows me and my team to allocate tasks dynamically, sharing them between us. It also allows us to review what's going on, shift priorities as needed and focus on what's in our control.

Over time I've also learned when to schedule productive time, and when to take time off. I've built things into my life that allow me to refocus, such as mediation and exercise. And I deliberately keep this time open for that important work. It's not 'productive' time in the same way we might normally view productivity, but it allows me to have the space and focus to give my business and clients the attention they deserve.

35 Weir, K. (2019). 'Give me a break. Psychologists explore the type and frequency of breaks we need to refuel our energy and enhance our well-being.' APA. Retrieved March 2, 2026 at https://www.apa.org/monitor/2019/01/break.

Productivity is not about squeezing more into the day – but it is about finding the space and time to create movement in your business. When you identify your priorities, minimise duplication, delegate intentionally and protect your energy, something important shifts. You stop feeling like you're spinning on a carousel and start directing your day, instead of feeling forced to react to it. And when you can direct your day, you can direct your business too.

Time will always be finite. You can't build more hours into your day. But when you decide, strategically, how to spend your time, and then fiercely protect it, you can transform it from a source of stress into a strategic asset.

Accelerate your progress

If you'd like to dive deeper into this, scan the QR code below to watch a short video where I discuss this chapter in more depth to allow you to create more space, structure and breathing room in your business.

Because success isn't just about getting more done. It's about creating a business and life that work for you too.

Chapter 11

Starting out as a new business owner

'If you don't build your dream, someone else will hire you to help them build theirs.' – Dhirubhai Ambani

In my work with clients, I'm often part of the conversation when they're thinking about starting a new business. While our focus and expertise is of course on the financial elements, this is all part of a single approach to starting a business. And, as a business owner myself, I've had to tackle this entire approach myself.

The thing is, starting a business is a bit like building a flat-pack bookshelf from Ikea. If you follow the steps in order, piece by piece, then it all comes together beautifully (even if you do need to take breaks for a cuppa now and again!). If you skip a step, however, you'll be stuck scratching your head and wondering why the whole thing wobbles.

This chapter is for those who have decided to start being their own boss, whether you've had an opportunity open up for you to be a contractor within an existing organisation, or you've decided to head out on your own as a sole trader or business owner, turning your side hustle into your main gig. Whatever the reason you have for starting your business, here's what we've learned (both on the financial side, and the business side) and what you need to know.

Your flat pack approach to setting up your business

Testing your bright idea

Most business owners first have a bright idea. You've seen a gap in the market, or something that you can do better or more competitively than anyone else, and now you want to start a business. That's fantastic. But before you rush forward to register a name and start a marketing strategy, you need to test your idea.

Build a real business plan and document how you think your business will work (there is a lot of information and even examples available online, and AI tools, such as ChatGPT will even create a template for you). Then speak to people you trust. This might be family, friends, colleagues or advisors. Ask them what they think and how they see this working. Listen to their advice and take it on board.

Remember that being your own boss isn't always easy. You're the final decision maker and the person that bears the ultimate responsibility for the obligations your business will have and the service or products you provide. So initially, your hours may move from a 40-hour week to a 75 or 80-hour week. It's not uncommon when you first start your business to do far more unpaid hours than you expect. In fact, A Wells Fargo/Gallup Small Business Index survey found 62% of small-business owners work 50 or more hours a week, with an average of 52 hours weekly.[36]

While we don't want this to be the case in the long run, it's often part and parcel of growing your business.

Tips to test your bright business idea

- If you still have a day job, don't give it up straight away. Work out a way that you can do both in the initial phases if it's possible.
- Don't forget to document how your cashflow will work in your business plan. This is a vital part of building a sustainable business.
- Be sure to ask yourself the tough questions. As the business takes off and develops, will you be able to handle it alone or will you need to hire staff? How will you do that? How much money do you need monthly to keep the business and yourself afloat? You don't have to know everything at the start of the process, but it helps to minimise the surprises that might crop up.

Know your own skillset

When it comes to running your own business, it's important to understand where you have skills or expertise, and where you might not. Knowing what you know, and doing it well, is what differentiates you within your business from your competitors. Even if they can do what you do, they aren't like you. You will offer something totally unique and different.

---

36 Jacobe, D. (2005). 'Work Is Labor of Love for Small-Business Owners.' Gallup. Retrieved March 9, 2026 at https://news.gallup.com/poll/18088/work-labor-love-smallbusiness-owners.aspx.

And when you're self-employed, knowing what you do know and what you don't allows you to be open to change so you can grow and evolve. When you can do this you'll also be open to learning, recognising what you don't know yet, and growing that knowledge and experience.

Being self employed is where I started. And for me, like for most other people who start out as self-employed, there comes a point in your business where you'll be pushed to ask yourself whether it's time to grow. Do you stay the size you are, with the revenue you have? Or do you look at alternatives, for example turn to contract work, go back into a company as an employee, work more hours yourself or look at ways you can systemise or outsource.

I elected to grow because I knew that what it would take to do this fell within my skillset. I documented my processes, hired staff, delegated some of my client workload and invested in Clickup to systemise recurring tasks. It's a cost but I see it as a necessary part of business that allows us to do what we need to do in an extraordinary way!

This might not be the right approach for you. But knowing your own skillset will help guide you in all the decisions in your business – whether it's finding your unique selling point or deciding when and how to scale and grow, and certainly when it's important to find others who can fill in the gaps in your own knowledge or experience.

Tips for knowing your own skillset

- Understand your strengths
- Know what you bring to the market
- Understand how you're different from your competitors
- Recognise what you don't know and be open to learning
- Be ready to outsource and systemise to fill in gaps in your own knowledge and skills

Setting up the business

This is the practical setup stage. And it's usually at this stage that I might come in to give some advice from a financial and business perspective, because your business structure will likely depend on the revenue you expect to generate. But there are some things you'll need to do first.

Decide on a business name and register it

First you'll want to decide on a business name if you're going to use one and register it. If you're going to operate as a sole trader, you can also choose to register this as your own name. The best way to do this is via the ASIC website. There are lots of companies that will register your business for you, and they look quite official on their websites. But you'll end up getting charged more if you go that route, and it's very easy to register directly via ASIC.[37]

Follow the process to check if the business name you'd like is available, and if so, apply to register it as the name of your business. If it's not available, you'll need to consider another name and go through the checking process again.

Decide on a business structure

This is the time to reach out and connect with your Accountant. The revenue you expect to make can impact the structure that makes the most sense for your business. Common business structures in Australia include:

- **Sole trader** – the simplest structure, where you operate the business in your own name or under a registered business name.

37 Australian Securities and Investments Commission. (2025). Register a company. https://www.asic.gov.au/for-business-and-companies/companies/register-a-company/.

- **Partnership** – where two or more people share ownership and responsibility for the business.
- **Company** – a separate legal entity that can provide different tax and liability outcomes.
- **Trust** – often used alongside a company to manage income distribution and asset protection.

Each structure has different tax implications, reporting requirements and responsibilities, so it's worth getting advice before you decide.

I've seen first-hand how important this can be. One of our clients helped his brother start a business in another state. They set it up quickly as a sole trader and the business took off far faster than anyone expected. In its first year it generated more than $400,000 in revenue and nearly $200,000 in profit.

The problem was that no professional advice had been sought when the business was established. By the time their accountant became involved during tax return preparation the following year, the structure was already in place and couldn't be changed retrospectively. For around 18 months the business continued operating as a sole trader, which meant a significant difference in the tax outcome.

Eventually the business was restructured into a company linked to a trust, with the brother becoming an employee of the company and receiving wages and super through payroll. But the lesson was clear – getting the structure right at the beginning can save a lot of headaches later.

It's also a good habit to check in with your accountant six to eight weeks before the end of the financial year. That allows time to review how your business is tracking and make adjustments if needed. And if something significant changes – like winning a contract that could double your revenue – that's another good moment to pick up the phone and get advice.

Your choice of business structure will have a knock-on effect too. Depending on your structure and expected revenue, you may need to register for:

- An ABN
- GST
- PAYG withholding, particularly if you hire staff
- Super obligations

Again, your accountant or advisor can guide you through this choice. It's always better to set this up correctly from the beginning rather than having to go back and fix this later.

Open a separate business bank account

One of the most important things you can do when starting a business is open a separate bank account. Keeping your business income and expenses separate from your personal spending makes bookkeeping far easier and helps you clearly see how your business is performing. Even if you've decided to operate as a sole trader, this separation is incredibly valuable. It avoids confusion, simplifies your tax preparation and helps your bookkeeper or accountant work more efficiently.

It also builds good habits from the start – treating your business as a business.

Select your software

Choose the software that you need to run your business. There are certain categories that you'll certainly want to consider. For example, your accounting software will be very important. But you'll also want to think about whether or not you need a CRM to systemise your workflows, something like ClickUp, Karbon or Asana. You'll also likely need a video conferencing service, a Google account and maybe another document management software. This could be as simple as using files in Word, or Google docs, or you might want something more comprehensive like Microsoft SharePoint. Of course, there are also specific types of software for certain industries, and you may need a subscription to this category as well.

Finally, consider whether you'll get an AI subscription. A general chat-based AI tool like ChatGPT, Copilot or Claude (which were the primary options at the time of publishing) is excellent for helping you research, create some types of content and even create basic marketing plans, for example. Perplexity, on the other hand, is fantastic at fact checking and researching, so if you're starting a business that needs this work, then it's a great choice.

Start tracking your business numbers

Once your software is set up and your business is ready to trade, it's time to start tracking your income and expenses. Often new business owners delay this because they believe their business is just too small to worry about the bookkeeping yet. But the earlier you start tracking your numbers, the easier everything becomes. And we already know how important it is to understand our numbers.

Even if you're only issuing a handful of invoices or paying a few expenses each month, building the habit of recording everything properly will save you a lot of time and headaches later.

Create a Business Playbook

When you first start a business everything feels new. You're trying to figure things out for the first time. You're probably trying different things and approaches, and seeing what works best for you. It can feel chaotic, but that's totally normal. However, once you do find something that works, and that you want to be able to repeat, you need to document that process right away.

Documenting your processes in what I like to call your 'Business Playbook' will make your life much easier. If you're anything like me you'll think, 'I'll remember that!' but when it comes time to do it again, you'll find that you've forgotten something important. Documenting it ensures that you don't waste your time or duplicate your efforts.

Your Business Playbook doesn't need to be complicated or formal. It can start as a simple document or folder where you record the steps you follow for the tasks you do regularly. For example, you might document:

- How you onboard new clients
- How you deliver your services or products
- How you invoice customers
- How you track work and follow up on outstanding tasks

At first this might feel unnecessary. After all, if you're the only person working in your business, you might already know all this. But documenting these processes allows you to see where you can streamline your processes, create consistency, save yourself time and energy and, importantly, allow you to easily train staff or contractors when you're ready to grow.

When mistakes happen, or you identify better ways to do things, be sure to review your processes so you can adjust them and improve them.

Engage with a good accountant and BAS agent

If you haven't already, be sure to engage with a BAS agent and accountant that you trust. Of course, in the early days, you may not have the funds to have a professional doing all your books. But once you grow and scale, outsourcing your bookkeeping is one of the best things you can do.

BAS agents have the skills to look after you and your business, and to take the stress out of the daily 'numbers' jobs. They can also help run reports, finalise invoices and even do payroll. As they become more familiar with the ins and outs of your business they'll become a valuable advisor in many aspects of your business.

If you already have a BAS agent, here are five key questions that I suggest you ask both yourself and your BAS agent to get the conversation started and allow you to better understand how your business is performing and identify any areas that might need attention.

1. Do I have a clear picture of how my business is performing right now? What report would we look at to answer this?
2. Are all of my bank accounts reconciled and are my BAS/IAS, super and payroll obligations up-to-date?
3. What are the top two or three red flags you see in my numbers right now?
4. What's one simple change we could make in the next 30 days to improve cashflow? What's one thing I'm doing well financially that I should keep doing?
5. If this was your business is there anything you'd do differently? What would you change and focus on in the next 90 days?

If you have the time, or maybe in a second conversation, I'd also ask, are there any apps or automations that you'd recommend that would make my life easier? Your advisors will know what will make your life easier!

If you're still looking for a financial advisor or BAS agent, start by asking your network or associates who they would recommend. And you can always reach out to me directly at keri@sortyourbooks.com.au and we can discuss some options of working with us or give you some ideas of those that are within my community that we can refer you to.

Build your business network

Running a business can sometimes feel like a lonely experience. When you're the owner, the responsibility ultimately sits with you. But you absolutely do not have to go through this journey on your own.

One of the most valuable things you can do as a business owner is build a network of people around you who understand the challenges of running a business. Think of this as building your tribe. These are the people who are walking a similar path to you and who can share ideas, insight, support and even opportunities along the way.

For lots of business owners, networking can feel uncomfortable at first. Turning up to a room full of strangers and introducing yourself can be intimidating. But it's like joining a gym. The first time might feel awkward, but once you've shown up a few times, you start recognising people, you'll understand the process, and the conversations become easier. And that's when the connections can start to grow.

There are many different types of networking groups. Some are quite formal, like BNI, while others are more casual, local arrangements. You can also find online communities if that's more your thing that connect business owners within your industry or local area.

The key is just to start somewhere. Go to a meeting, introduce yourself and be open to making connections with new people. You may not find the right group straight away, and that's perfectly normal. But don't give up until you find one where you feel comfortable and connected.

The benefits of networking with other business owners go far beyond just finding new clients. It also allows you to:

- Learn what's working for others
- Share ideas and experiences
- Gain referrals and partnerships
- Build confidence in your business decisions
- Develop a support network of people who understand the journey you're on

I've seen these benefits in my own business. During a local networking event I connected with a business owner who now runs two businesses that we support on a regular basis. We've also introduced other clients to the same networking group because it's a safe and welcoming space for business owners to meet, learn and support each other.

Sometimes challenges in business can feel enormous when you're facing them alone. But when you're surrounded by others working towards similar goals, those challenges become far easier to navigate.

As journalist and author Tracey Spicer puts it: 'Sometimes challenges seem enormous, but if you can connect with others working towards the same goal, it becomes more achievable.'

I don't always get to attend as many events as I'd like. But whenever I do go, I always come away with valuable conversations, new ideas and connections that strengthen my business and our entire business community.

Building your business – one step at a time

Starting a business can feel exciting, overwhelming and everything in between. In this chapter we've looked at some of the key foundations that can help you get started – testing your idea, understanding your skillset, setting up the right structure, putting systems in place and building good financial habits from the very beginning.

Just like assembling that flat-pack bookshelf, the goal is to take things one step at a time. When you follow a process and build the right foundations early, your business has a much better chance of standing strong as it grows.

Of course, this chapter isn't intended to give you every answer or replace professional advice. Every business is different, and the decisions that are right for one person may not be right for another. Think of these ideas as a starting point – practical suggestions to help you think about how you want to set up and run your business.

As you move forward, take the time to do your own research and speak with people who can provide advice specific to your situation. This might include an accountant, bookkeeper, lawyer, business coach or trusted members of your professional network. Surrounding yourself with the right people and being open to learning from others will make the journey much easier.

Being in business requires confidence in what you offer, but it also requires humility. None of us knows everything, and the most successful business owners are the ones who stay curious, ask questions and remain open to improving how they operate.

Starting a business is rarely a straight line. There will be lessons, adjustments and plenty of learning along the way. But with the right foundations, good advice and a willingness to keep improving, you give yourself the best possible chance to build something strong, sustainable and rewarding.

Chapter 12

Where to from here?

By now, you've seen just how important your numbers really are. Not just at tax time, or when something goes wrong, but to help empower you to make quick, strategic decisions that can truly shape and grow your business.

Having this understanding doesn't just mean that you feel more confident (though it should do this as well). It also shapes how you show up in your business, because you know what's really happening, you trust that you have the information you need and you're able to guide where you go to from here.

That sense of control is something that many business owners have lost, even if they don't realise it. And when you get it back because you understand your numbers, then you can move out of reacting to whatever is thrown at you. Instead, you can start to see patterns, you can plan ahead and you can make decisions early and well (before things become a problem!).

That shift is where things will really begin to change for you and for your business. And if I've left you with that, then I think I've done my job.

But I do want to talk about one more thing – and that's to remind you that you don't have to start by making major business overhauls or use all your resources getting the latest software or build AI agents to automate everything in your business. This would just leave you more stretched than ever. Instead, you just need to focus on doing the ordinary well, but doing it well consistently.

Doing the ordinary well

In business I've found that success rarely comes from doing one big thing perfectly. It comes from doing the ordinary things well, over and over again.

It's a bit like keeping your kitchen floor clean. It's not exciting, and it's certainly not the reason you bought your house, but when it's done regularly it changes how the whole space feels. The same applies in your business. Reviewing your numbers, following your processes, staying on top of your obligations and checking in on your cashflow might not feel like big moves, but they are the things that create stability and momentum over time.

When you take ownership of these everyday tasks and approach them with intention and consistency, things start to feel more manageable. You're no longer relying on memory or trying to work things out from scratch each time. You rely on your processes, you trust your numbers, you have systems and solutions in place and that makes your business easier to run.

It also makes it easier to grow. If something only exists in your head, it's difficult to repeat and almost impossible to hand over to someone else. When your processes are documented and your systems are in place, you create a foundation that allows your business to expand without everything falling back onto you.

So don't worry if you don't have the newest, shiniest AI agents automating your end of year tasks (for example). Just take what you have, and use it well, to support your business day in and day out.

You don't have to do this alone

And remember, you don't have to have all the answers yourself. This book is a great start, but it's also important to know when to ask for help. Surround yourself with people who care about your business and can support you. This might be a bookkeeper, an accountant, a business advisor or someone in your network who has been through similar experiences. These people don't just help you with tasks. They help you see things differently, ask better questions and make more informed decisions.

Sometimes that support will come with a price tag, and that can feel uncomfortable when you're starting out. But the right advice at the right time can save you far more in the long run, whether that's time, money or stress.

This is just the beginning

This book isn't about turning you into an accountant. It's about helping you feel more confident in your business and more comfortable understanding what's going on behind the scenes.

Some of what we've covered might feel simple, and that's intentional. In business, it's often the basics that make the biggest difference. When you build the habit of checking in on your numbers and understanding what they mean, everything else becomes easier to manage.

If there's one thing I'd encourage you to do after reading this book, it's to take action. Log into your accounting software and check out your reports. Book a chat with your bookkeeper or accountant. Make it a regular thing, monthly or quarterly, and calendar some time to check your numbers and ask a few of the questions that we've covered.

You won't be perfect at first, and everyone's first step will look different. But just take it – even if it feels awkward. Progress in business doesn't come from knowing what to do, it comes from actually doing it.

Accelerate your progress

Accelerate your progress, scan the QR code below to watch a short video where I discuss and summarise the book and what you've read to sort your books, sort your business, sort your life!

Working together

If you'd like support putting this into practice, I can also help. That's what I do – work with business owners to help them understand their numbers, build better financial habits and feel more confident in the decisions they're making.

If you'd like to have a conversation, you can reach out to me directly at: keri@keriwhitelaw.com.au. For more tips, insights and practical advice for business owners, visit www.keriwhitelaw.com.au or use the QR codes below to connect with me through my website and social media channels.

LINKEDIN INSTAGRAM FACEBOOK

About the author

With more than 25 years supporting small-medium businesses across multiple industries, Keri specialises in connection and building good relationships with her clients. She has helped hundreds of business owners clean up their data, understand their obligations and make informed financial decisions without stress.

Known for her warm, grounded, relationship-first approach, Keri helps clients feel safe to ask questions, sort through the messy bits and finally understand what's really going on behind the scenes. Her work spans break-even analysis (your 'magic number'), cash flow management, compliance oversight, payroll support and building bookkeeping systems that actually work in the real world and support your life, not make you feel swallowed up in it.

Over the years, Keri has helped hundreds of business owners clean up their data, understand their obligations and make clear, confident financial decisions without stress, shame, or confusing jargon. Often referred to as the 'accountant interpreter' by clients, she makes sense of what her clients are being told.

Her goal is to help you strengthen your financial foundations and create sustainable momentum – with a little more ease, a little more intention and a lot more confidence. And when your business is strong, your life is too.

Sort your books. Sort your business. Sort your life.

www.ingramcontent.com/pod-product-compliance
Lightning Source LLC
LaVergne TN
LVHW050915210926
848482LV00012B/451
9781764251334